Llewellyn's

Witches' Datebook

2024

Featuring

Art by Jennifer Hewitson
Text by Elizabeth Barrette, Deborah Blake,
Monica Crosson, Kelden, James Kambos, Mickie Mueller,
Melissa Tipton, JD Walker, Tess Whitehurst,
and Laurel Woodward

ISBN 978-0-7387-6904-2

2024

JANUARY
S M T W T F S
1 2 3 4 5 6
7 8 9 10 11 12 13
14 15 16 17 18 19 20
21 22 23 24 25 26 27
28 29 30 31

FEBRUARY
S M T W T F S
1 2 3
4 5 6 7 8 9 10
11 12 13 14 15 16 17
18 19 20 21 22 23 24
25 26 27 28 29

MARCH
S M T W T F S
1 2
3 4 5 6 7 8 9
10 11 12 13 14 15 16
17 18 19 20 21 22 23
24 25 26 27 28 29 30
31

APRIL
S M T W T F S
1 2 3 4 5 6
7 8 9 10 11 12 13
14 15 16 17 18 19 20
21 22 23 24 25 26 27
28 29 30

MAY
S M T W T F S
1 2 3 4
5 6 7 8 9 10 11
12 13 14 15 16 17 18
19 20 21 22 23 24 25
26 27 28 29 30 31

JUNE
S M T W T F S
1
2 3 4 5 6 7 8
9 10 11 12 13 14 15
16 17 18 19 20 21 22
23 24 25 26 27 28 29
30

JULY
S M T W T F S
1 2 3 4 5 6
7 8 9 10 11 12 13
14 15 16 17 18 19 20
21 22 23 24 25 26 27
28 29 30 31

AUGUST
S M T W T F S
1 2 3
4 5 6 7 8 9 10
11 12 13 14 15 16 17
18 19 20 21 22 23 24
25 26 27 28 29 30 31

SEPTEMBER
S M T W T F S
1 2 3 4 5 6 7
8 9 10 11 12 13 14
15 16 17 18 19 20 21
22 23 24 25 26 27 28
29 30

OCTOBER
S M T W T F S
1 2 3 4 5
6 7 8 9 10 11 12
13 14 15 16 17 18 19
20 21 22 23 24 25 26
27 28 29 30 31

NOVEMBER
S M T W T F S
1 2
3 4 5 6 7 8 9
10 11 12 13 14 15 16
17 18 19 20 21 22 23
24 25 26 27 28 29 30

DECEMBER
S M T W T F S
1 2 3 4 5 6 7
8 9 10 11 12 13 14
15 16 17 18 19 20 21
22 23 24 25 26 27 28
29 30 31

2025

JANUARY
S M T W T F S
1 2 3 4
5 6 7 8 9 10 11
12 13 14 15 16 17 18
19 20 21 22 23 24 25
26 27 28 29 30 31

FEBRUARY
S M T W T F S
1
2 3 4 5 6 7 8
9 10 11 12 13 14 15
16 17 18 19 20 21 22
23 24 25 26 27 28

MARCH
S M T W T F S
1
2 3 4 5 6 7 8
9 10 11 12 13 14 15
16 17 18 19 20 21 22
23 24 25 26 27 28 29
30 31

APRIL
S M T W T F S
1 2 3 4 5
6 7 8 9 10 11 12
13 14 15 16 17 18 19
20 21 22 23 24 25 26
27 28 29 30

MAY
S M T W T F S
1 2 3
4 5 6 7 8 9 10
11 12 13 14 15 16 17
18 19 20 21 22 23 24
25 26 27 28 29 30 31

JUNE
S M T W T F S
1 2 3 4 5 6 7
8 9 10 11 12 13 14
15 16 17 18 19 20 21
22 23 24 25 26 27 28
29 30

JULY
S M T W T F S
1 2 3 4 5
6 7 8 9 10 11 12
13 14 15 16 17 18 19
20 21 22 23 24 25 26
27 28 29 30 31

AUGUST
S M T W T F S
1 2
3 4 5 6 7 8 9
10 11 12 13 14 15 16
17 18 19 20 21 22 23
24 25 26 27 28 29 30
31

SEPTEMBER
S M T W T F S
1 2 3 4 5 6
7 8 9 10 11 12 13
14 15 16 17 18 19 20
21 22 23 24 25 26 27
28 29 30

OCTOBER
S M T W T F S
1 2 3 4
5 6 7 8 9 10 11
12 13 14 15 16 17 18
19 20 21 22 23 24 25
26 27 28 29 30 31

NOVEMBER
S M T W T F S
1
2 3 4 5 6 7 8
9 10 11 12 13 14 15
16 17 18 19 20 21 22
23 24 25 26 27 28 29
30

DECEMBER
S M T W T F S
1 2 3 4 5 6
7 8 9 10 11 12 13
14 15 16 17 18 19 20
21 22 23 24 25 26 27
28 29 30 31

Editing and layout by Lauryn Heineman

Cover illustration and interior art © Jennifer Hewitson

Art on chapter openings © Jennifer Hewitson

Astrological calculations compiled and programmed by Rique Pottenger, based on the earlier work of Neil F. Michelsen.

Printed in China

Table of Contents

How to Use Llewellyn's Witches' Datebook

Welcome to *Llewellyn's 2024 Witches' Datebook*! This datebook was designed especially for Witches, Pagans, and magical people. Use it to plan sabbat celebrations, magic, Full Moon rites, and even dentist and doctor appointments. At right is a symbol key to some of the features of this datebook.

Moon Quarters: The Moon's cycle is divided into four quarters, which are noted in the weekly pages along with their exact times. When the Moon changes quarter, both quarters are listed, as well as the time of the change. In addition, a symbol for the new quarter is placed where the numeral for the date usually appears.

Moon in the Signs: Approximately every two and a half days, the Moon moves from one zodiac sign to the next. The sign that the Moon is in at the beginning of the day (midnight Eastern Time) is noted next to the quarter listing. If the Moon changes signs that day, there will be a notation saying "☽ enters" followed by the symbol for the sign it is entering.

Moon Void-of-Course: Just before the Moon enters a new sign, it will make one final aspect (angular relationship) to another planet. Between that last aspect and the entrance of the Moon into the next sign it is said to be void-of-course. Activities begun when the Moon is void-of-course rarely come to fruition, or they turn out very differently than planned.

Planetary Movement: When a planet or asteroid moves from one sign into another, this change (called an *ingress*) is noted on the calendar pages with the exact time. The Moon and Sun are considered planets in this case. The planets (except for the Sun and Moon) can also appear to move backward as seen from Earth. This is called a *planetary retrograde*, and is noted on the calendar pages with the symbol ℞. When the planet begins to move forward, or direct, again, it is marked D, and the time is also noted.

Planting and Harvesting Days: The best days for planting and harvesting are noted on the calendar pages with a seedling icon (planting) and a basket icon (harvesting).

Time Zone Changes: The times and dates of all astrological phenomena in this datebook are based on Eastern Time. If you live outside the Eastern Time zone, you will need to make the following changes: Pacific Time subtract three hours; Mountain Time subtract two hours; Central Time subtract one hour; Alaska subtract four hours; and Hawaii subtract five hours. All data is adjusted for Daylight Saving Time.

Planets

☉	Sun	♅	Uranus
☽	Moon	♆	Neptune
☿	Mercury	♇	Pluto
♀	Venus	⚷	Chiron
♂	Mars		
♃	Jupiter		
♄	Saturn		

Signs

♈	Aries	♐	Sagittarius
♉	Taurus	♑	Capricorn
♊	Gemini	♒	Aquarius
♋	Cancer	♓	Pisces
♌	Leo		
♍	Virgo		
♎	Libra		
♏	Scorpio		

Motion

℞ Retrograde
D Direct

1st Quarter/New Moon ☽ 3rd Quarter/Full Moon ☺

2nd Quarter ☽ 4th Quarter ☽

Activate Your Witch Sight
by Melissa Tipton

Witches skirt the boundaries of the known, the predictable, the commonplace, seeking the strange and wonderful mysteries hidden within the mundane. This ability to see what is often overlooked means that Witches have access to creative solutions, opportunities, and alternative pathways to growth. To strengthen this ability—what I call "witch sight"—we'll explore daily life practices that help us see beyond the ordinary before concluding with a sight-enhancing spell.

Breaking Out of Mental Ruts

Getting curious about mental grooves or energetic patterns that limit our ability to see fresh possibilities is a wonderful way to enhance witch sight, and we can do this by investigating how we make meaning of our life experiences. For every event, there are as many interpretations as there are people to experience it. We each create our own meaning, which indicates that, to a large extent, meaning is fluid—in other words, it's an ideal medium for magic making.

Are there meanings that you frequently encounter in your life? For instance, do you find yourself thinking that other people aren't very supportive, that you give more than you receive in relationships? Or perhaps it seems like you simply can't get ahead. For every positive step forward, you stumble two steps back. These regularly recurring meanings are important themes in the story of your life, and they help you assess whether you're living the story you want to be living or if it's time to rewrite the narrative. If your themes feel frustrating or limiting, becoming aware of them is the first step in finding ways to unravel old patterns and initiate change.

I find journaling to be the best practice for noticing themes, and you might choose to keep a separate journal for this exercise to make it even easier to flip through past entries and spot patterns. Make a note of interactions or situations that trigger an unpleasant emotional reaction. This can be as simple as jotting down a few bullet points, so don't fret if you don't have time for epic journaling sessions every day. The main details you want to record are how you felt and what meaning you took away from the experience.

It might help to imagine you're telling a friend what you learned from the situation, boiling it down to the essentials. For example, "This just goes to show, I can't trust bosses/men/etc.," "Every time I let people know who I really am, they pull away," or "If you want to get ahead, you have to (fill in the blank)." Don't worry if recurring threads aren't visible right away. This can take time, and the spell we'll be getting to shortly is designed to make this detective work even easier.

Healing Your Ancestral Stories

When you do notice a theme, ask yourself if you've witnessed this before in your family, whether through direct observation or through stories about your relatives and ancestors. Often, our key themes have been inherited, and as Witches, we're in a powerful position to use our magic to heal ancestral trauma and interrupt patterns that no longer serve us. By engaging with any of the practices in this article, you're redirecting energy into new channels, creating pathways of possibility not only for yourself, but also for the people around you. How often have you been inspired to change after watching someone else do things differently? We can all serve as expanders for each other, demonstrating new ways of being in the world.

A friend once learned from a spirit guide that when we work to heal something in our family line, this is like shining an energetic flashlight on the area, making it easier for everyone, living and passed, to heal this issue if they so choose. I love this way of looking at things! It conjures up an image of the Witch in a magical library, turning on a reading lamp within the family's energy field, helping everyone see and access greater healing and freedom.

Shifting Patterns in Daily Life

Another way to shift a theme is to witness when it's being activated in the moment. For instance, let's say you've identified the theme of "If I don't do things perfectly, I'll be rejected." You sent an email to a coworker, but it's been a few days and they haven't replied. While eating lunch, you realize you've been so distracted that half your sandwich is gone and you barely remember eating it. As you introduce curiosity, you notice your mind has been caught in a loop, replaying everything in your email, picking it apart for any "mistakes" that might be causing your coworker to "reject you."

Aha! Since you've done the work of noticing this pattern in your journaling, this makes it easier to spot when it's cropping up in daily life. You think, "Well, it's weird that Kai hasn't responded yet, but then again, I know this sort of thing tends to get my hackles up. Hmm . . . is it possible that Kai's just busy and this isn't a rejection?" Even if you still feel pretty convinced of the old meaning, you're already shifting the cycle by introducing a sliver of healthy skepticism.

I like to ask myself, "What else might be true in this situation?" This question is less about identifying with total certainty what's happening and why and more about brainstorming alternative meanings, even if some of them feel a little far-fetched. Think of it as warming up your witch sight, making it easier to see outside the box. For example, maybe Kai hasn't replied because they're drowning in other work projects, or they're having a rough week at home, or they've run off and joined the circus. Who knows!

Witches of lore are known for living in the liminal, and we can walk in their magical footsteps by embracing the in-betweens and the maybes. While the ego battles to attain certainty, often at the expense of happiness or accuracy, witch sight invites us to question our thoughts; to expand our perspective; to ask, "I wonder if . . . ?" This willingness to see things differently rewrites stubborn patterns, one moment of curiosity at a time.

Choosing to Repattern Your Energy

Another potent daily life practice for shifting unwanted themes is challenging ourselves to choose differently when we notice a theme is active. Continuing our previous example with Kai the coworker, after you've introduced the possibility that Kai's delayed response doesn't mean you're being rejected, you can further shake up the energy of this old pattern by identifying one choice you can make that's different from what you might have done before.

For instance, let's say when you've found yourself in this situation in the past, you sent another email the very next day, hoping to prompt an immediate response. Or perhaps you vented to another coworker that Kai is taking too long to get back to you. This time, what's something you can do differently, however small it might seem?

You don't have to completely revise your approach; simply choose one thing to alter. Maybe you opt not to send that follow-up email yet, giving Kai some breathing room. Or perhaps when you find yourself stressing about Kai's sluggish response, you make a conscious effort to practice self-care instead of fully following the path of anxious thoughts. You might give yourself a mini scalp massage or take a two-minute break to Google cute puppy pics. Like a cascade of energetic dominoes, these tiny changes can initiate far-reaching effects.

A Spell to Enhance Your Witch Sight

The following spell is designed to supercharge your witch sight, and it's best performed on the Full Moon.

You will need:

- Optional: 1 tsp. dried herbs, choosing from chamomile, eyebright, or mugwort (If you have ragweed allergies, I don't recommend using chamomile.)
- Bowl, ideally glass or silver-colored metal
- Spring or purified water
- Cloth that can be dipped in water, large enough that you can drape it over your eyes
- Strainer if using herbs

If using, place 1 teaspoon of dried herbs in the bowl, then fill with 2 to 3 cups of spring or purified water. Place the bowl in the moonlight, and with your palms hovering above the water, chant the following, feeling the energy of the spell streaming from your hands into the bowl:

I call upon the Witch's Moon
To help me see with eyes anew.
Patterns, truths, and hidden paths
Are all revealed by silvery light.
I hereby activate my witch sight!
So mote it be.

Dip the cloth in the water (optionally, you can strain the herbs from the water first), wringing it out so it's well moistened but not dripping wet. Lie back comfortably and place the cloth over closed eyes, feeling the energy of the moonlit water activating your power of witch sight.

When you're done, strain the herbs from the liquid and compost or discard, or simply pour the water onto the earth.

Morning Rituals for the Busy Witch

by Mickie Mueller

Good morning! It's true that some mornings are better than others, but what if you had a way to have more actual good mornings? A morning ritual can set the tone for your day. I'm not talking about something complex, because who has time to add anything extra to your morning? I know, you're already busy, but I've got some simple ways to add magic, beauty, and peace to your morning so that when you head out into the world, you feel empowered to face your day by meeting the challenges and recognizing the blessings.

We might think of a ritual as a really large practice—casting a circle, treading the compass, tracing pentagrams in the air, and setting up an altar with statues, offerings, and candles—but let's rethink the idea of what a ritual can look like. A ritual can be any mindful action or series of actions that you repeat to help you connect with the spiritual part of yourself. It can be a way to bless yourself and the day ahead and get your head into a healthy frame of mind, and it can carry you throughout your whole day.

I used to look at the news and social media first thing in the morning, but I realized that starting off my day with internal messages instead of a barrage of external messages was better for my general well-being. I do grab my phone first thing, but only to open an app to do my morning meditation before my feet hit the floor. A five-minute guided meditation can really shift my day. Even if you don't like to meditate, you can still take a moment to set intentions for the day and practice some mindfulness. You can check the news and social media later, but try making your first thoughts of the day just for you.

Quick Morning Mindfulness

You can do this sitting on your bed or while you're still lying down if you prefer. You might want to set your alarm five to ten minutes earlier to incorporate a few minutes of mindfulness in the morning. I promise it's worth it.

First, do a few cycles of deep breathing. Filling your lungs with air in a purposeful manner is a powerful way to bring mindfulness into your morning and trains your nervous system to handle stress throughout your day. I like to use a method called box breathing. It's easy to do because all you need to remember is the number four. Breathe in deeply for four seconds, hold four seconds, breathe out four seconds, hold for four seconds, and repeat. You can even commit to four rounds of this breath if you wish. Four is a number of stability and control, corresponding to the four elements and the four cardinal directions. That makes a fourfold breath a perfectly magical way to start the day.

After some conscious deep breathing, take a moment to check in with yourself. Ask yourself how you're feeling. Are you tired, well rested, excited about the day, or a little nervous? There is no wrong answer. Feel the feelings and try your best to acknowledge them without judgment. We feel how we feel, so just allow yourself to rest in this space for a moment.

After a quick check-in, you may simply have a short series of statements of your intention for the day. You can try something like these:

I have the power to make my day great.
My magic is with me today.
I am shielded from all energy not aligned with me.

Personalize these and make them things that are important to you, things you're working on in your life, work, and magic. You can write them down and keep them next to your bed to repeat every morning. As goals and challenges in your life change, you can adjust your affirmations accordingly.

Shower of Power

Water is an element that is cleansing, purifying, and healing, not just for our bodies, but for our spirit. Whether you take a shower every morning or a few times a week, you can use a quick water cleanse as part of your morning ritual. One of my favorite "no tools" rituals is done in my shower. Shower as usual, but at the end of your shower as the water pours over you, imagine any stress, psychic sludge from others, or lower vibrational energies from the previous day that you want to release coming out of your body and onto the surface of your skin. If you have a hard time visualizing, you can just say the words "I release yesterday's stress from my body" or something similar. Now switch your water to cooler or cold water. Let the water wash it all down the drain, never to return. Once you feel lighter and unburdened, imagine that the water forms a shining armor all over your body as you soak it up into your skin cells. When you turn off the shower, simply state, "I am cleansed and shielded."

Another very simple but powerful morning ritual is to splash your face with cold water, activating your senses. You can also use this practice to bless yourself by simply saying,

> I bless my eyes and all they see.
> I bless my ears and all they hear.
> I bless my mouth and all its words.
> I bless my nose and every breath.
> I bless my hands and all they touch.
> I bless my intuition; may it always guide me true.

There are other benefits to the cold-water face splash; it makes your skin all lovely and glowing, it can give you a much-needed boost of energy, and it's really good for your mental health. That cold water activates the vagus nerve, gives you a little endorphin boost, and resets your parasympathetic nervous system.* Congratulations, you now are better prepared to handle the stress you might face today. Repeating this as a daily ritual boosts the effects exponentially.

Your Magical Mug

Do you prefer coffee, tea, or some other beverage in the morning? Maybe you make it yourself or you get it on the go. Either way, a special

---

* Manuela Jungmann et al., "Effects of Cold Stimulation on Cardiac-Vagal Activation in Healthy Participants: Randomized Controlled Trial." *JMIR Formative Research* 2, no. 2 (2018): e10257, doi:10.2196/10257.

magical mug is another tool to create a morning ritual, and you can set it up the night before.

Grab your favorite mug—doesn't matter what kind it is as long as you love it and it feels special to you. Maybe it looks very witchy, is shaped like a cauldron, or has a botanical print, a special quote, or your favorite deity printed on it. All that matters is that you love it and love drinking out of it.

Make sure your mug is clean the night before and set it wherever you'll easily find it in the morning. Use a quartz crystal or any stone that matches the energy you want to manifest the next day. Hold that stone in your hands. Imagine your day filled with good choices, fortunate opportunities, loving conversations, and doors opening up to you, and allow that energy to fill the crystal. Place the crystal in your cup overnight, and it will adjust the energy of your cup while you sleep. The next morning, remove the crystal and fill your cup in the way that you usually do, in your own kitchen or by your favorite barista. You are ready to drink in the magic.

Candlelight Breakfast

I've discovered that lighting a small jar candle while I eat my breakfast, even if it's a quick breakfast, helps me be more in the moment and taste the sweetness of life.

If you want to use a scented jar candle, I suggest that you use a scent that won't clash with the scent of the food you usually eat for breakfast. An herb or spice scent can work well, but you might want to consider an unscented candle for this. You can add a homemade or store-bought sticker to the jar to represent a good day ahead, perhaps a sun for success, an eye for wakefulness or protection, or a heart to remind you to speak and act in as loving a way as possible. Make it something that you will probably want to magically bring into every day on a long-term basis. I suggest that you charge the candle with your intention ahead of time and also intend that it will continue to release the energy every time it's lit.

Keep your charged morning candle and a lighter or matches wherever you usually eat breakfast. That way, it's ready to go every morning and you don't have disrupt the practical chores of getting ready to keep your ritual going strong. Light it when you sit down for breakfast and extinguish it according to your tradition when you're finished.

These are just a few easy ways that you can create a simple morning ritual that adds value to your life every singe day. I hope you take these ideas, get creative with them, think of ways to incorporate them into your daily routine, and have a really good morning!

Practicing the Craft with Others
by Deborah Blake

For many of us, Witchcraft is primarily a solitary and deeply personal endeavor. There is a certain freedom in following a spiritual path that doesn't require attendance at a church or the presence of anyone other than yourself. But it can also sometimes be a lonely path to walk, living as we do in a society where Paganism is often poorly understood or not well accepted. So there are times when being able to gather with other Witches can give us a joy and companionship that takes our magical work to an entirely different level.

Unlike many Witches who came to Witchcraft on their own, my personal journey began with a study group/coven. I was invited to attend a Samhain ritual by the high priestess who ran the group, and it was there that I discovered that I was a Witch. (Surprise!) Because of this, my practice has always been a mixture of solitary and group work, and I eventually started my own coven, Blue Moon Circle, in spring 2004. Blue Moon Circle still exists, although it has gone through many changes over the years, and its core members are as close—or closer, in some cases—as family.

Our approach to ritual has altered somewhat over time, as we've become more eclectic and more flexible, but our commitment to the God and Goddess, our spiritual practice, and each other has remained the same. Here are some of the things I've learned in my years of practicing both with my own group and with others, as well as some helpful hints for a shared practice over the course of the year.

Five "To-Dos" When Practicing with Others

Whether you are working with your own coven, joining another group, or taking part in a ritual at a convention or festival, here are some things to keep in mind while sharing ritual space with other people.

1. Respect sacred space. Once the circle is cast, focus on the magical work being done, keep chatting to a minimum, and do your best to participate with an open mind and heart.

2. Respect others. Not everyone has the same level of experience or comfort with physicality, and everyone brings their own issues into circle. Treat everyone with kindness, respect personal boundaries (don't hug people you don't know without asking permission, for example), and do your best to accept those you are practicing with without judgment.

3. Remember the importance of focus and intent. No matter what kind of magical work you are doing, when you are practicing with others, the success or failure of the ritual will depend to a great extent on everyone being willing and able to put their full focus, intent, and energy into the work.

4. Perfect love and perfect trust are at the core of Witchcraft practiced with others. This refers back to points two and three. The people you do ritual with may not be your best friends. You may never even have met them before. But once you are inside circle, in sacred space, we try to gather "in perfect love and perfect trust." Because magical work requires a certain dropping of our normal defenses, we need to be able to trust that the person standing next to us will be accepting and also that we can depend on them to do their part. You may find that there is something wonderful about being in a space so filled with love.

5. Don't forget to have fun. While it is true that rituals can be very serious and meaningful, they are also happy gatherings with people who share your basic beliefs. It is said that we practice "with reverence and mirth," and I have definitely found this to be true with my own coven. It is important to take the magic seriously, but don't forget to enjoy being able to practice with others.

Group Witchcraft throughout the Year

There are various reasons to gather with a group of Witches, but the most common of those are esbats (Full Moons) and sabbats (the eight holidays that make up the Wheel of the Year). Here are a few suggestions for shared practice through the year, any of which can be as relaxed and spontaneous or as formal as you choose to make them.

Full Moon: It is always wonderful to celebrate the Full Moon outside, where you can stand under its glow and feel the touch of the Goddess on your skin. If the weather or circumstances don't allow it, inside is fine too. Light small candles to represent the glow of the Moon, chant, and/or have someone recite either "The Charge of the Goddess" or some other meaningful poem. Full Moons are powerful nights, and you can use them to perform magic or simply celebrate being Witches.

Imbolc: This sabbat, which falls on February 2, celebrates the first subtle stirring of spring, even though in many parts of the country we are still firmly in the grip of winter. It is a good time to start making plans for your goals for the year to come, whether magical or mundane, and your group can do spellwork for guidance or for success in whatever it is you hope to achieve. It is also traditional to use this sabbat for cleansing and purification rituals, so you start the new year out fresh.

Spring Equinox: On or around March 21, we mark the actual arrival of spring, no matter what the weather looks like outside your window. This sabbat is the perfect time to do magic for new beginnings. One easy magical ritual is to plant seeds, either outside or in a small pot indoors, to symbolize those things you wish to grow and flourish in the seasons to come.

Beltane: May Day, which falls on the first of May, is a holiday dedicated to love and fertility (whether literal or metaphorical). It is traditional to dance around the maypole, but if you can't do that, try hanging ribbons on a May bush or even a large houseplant. Write your wishes for love or anything else on your ribbon, and channel your group energy into the joy of the day.

Summer Solstice: On or around June 21, we celebrate the start of summer. This sabbat is full of energy, as it takes place on the longest day of the year. If you can, have a ritual outside under the Sun. This is the perfect time for magical work toward abundance, prosperity, and growth of any kind.

Lammas: Also known as Lughnasadh in honor of Lugh, the Celtic god of light, this holiday falls on August 1 and is the first of the three Pagan harvest festivals. It is specifically dedicated to grains, so if your group includes someone who bakes, be sure to share a loaf of bread together. (Or buy one from a local bakery. It's the sharing that counts.)

Mabon: The autumn equinox falls on or around September 21, and it is the second harvest festival. It is also one of only two days of the year when the light and the dark are equal, so it is the perfect time to do magical work for balance. (Who couldn't use more of that?)

Samhain: On October 31, we celebrate the witchiest holiday of them all, when the veil between the worlds is thin. As a group, you can create an altar for those you have lost (either in the past year or before), decorate it with pictures or mementos, and light candles in their honor.

Yule: The winter solstice falls on or around December 21. It is the perfect time to celebrate with family and friends, if your group is comfortable doing that, or to simply exchange small gifts and wishes for the coming year.

No matter how you choose to do it, practicing Witchcraft with others can be rewarding, fun, and deeply moving. Never underestimate the power of Witches when they gather, because when we come together as one, it is magic indeed.

Crystals for Divine Alignment
by Tess Whitehurst

In science, a crystal is defined by its unique arrangement or structure of atoms. In magic, it's helpful to be aware that each crystal also emanates a particular energetic structure. I sense it as a sort of three-dimensional sacred geometry of light that can be directed toward a person, place, or situation in a way that will amplify and enhance any given magical intention. When you pair an awareness of this energetic dynamic with the conscious choice to channel divine energy and power into your intention, your crystal work becomes exponentially more effective.

Of course, the conscious choice to channel divine energy and power into an intention is always something that will enhance your magical work, whether or not crystals are involved. Invoking divine energy not only supercharges your magic, but it also helps attune the outcome of your magic to the big picture. That is, it helps bring about not just what your human self thinks should happen, but what the part of you that is one with everything knows will be for your ultimate good, as well as the ultimate good of everyone concerned.

Crystals—and especially certain crystals, like the ones you'll read about—are particularly suited to help bring about a strong energetic restructuring that aligns your magic with whatever is for your purest and truest good, as well as the purest and truest good of all.

When you work with crystals, it will add a layer of mastery to your magic when you go beyond thinking of a stone as useful for a basic intention, such as "drawing wealth" or "opening the heart to love."

Instead, consider the systemic energetic restructuring that occurs when you enlist a crystal to positively affect your life experience. Think of crystal work as a way of opening up a channel to universal life force energy while creating the vibrational shifts within and around you that will allow your intentions to catch on, take root, and naturally expand in the deepest, best, and most all-encompassing possible ways. It's like you're changing your invisible energetic structure in such a way that your intentions can't help but manifest. By internalizing the vibrational quality of health (for example), all your cells and molecules shift, until you absolutely radiate well-being on every level. From this place, you just can't help but thrive. This is the magical dynamic crystals allow you to employ.

I know this all might sound a little arcane when you're just reading it on paper, but you'll get an idea of what I mean when you experience crystalline divine alignment for yourself. While all crystals can be employed for divine alignment, here are some excellent crystals to get you started.

Amber

Amber, a fossilized resin, often resembles golden honey but sometimes appears with tints of green, pink, or blue. Amber helps heal the body, mind, and spirit by bringing subtle, invisible vibrations into ideal harmony and resonance. If a condition, situation, relationship, or mood feels indefinably "off," amber can be employed to work on the energetic level to create the desired change.

Consciously enlist amber to help bring sweetness, joy, well-being, abundance, harmony, or success to any life area.

To work with amber for divine alignment, first go outside, hold it in your open palm, and bathe it in sunlight for a minute or two. Then hold it to your heart with both hands. Breathe and conjure up as much of a sense of inner well-being and harmony as you can. Direct this energy into the amber and imagine the stone sending its unique healing properties to whatever it is that you'd like it to align: your physical body, your mental or emotional health, or a particular situation or relationship.

Blue Calcite

Blue calcite is an energy healer and helps the body remember and rediscover its natural state of radiant well-being. It relieves stress by helping you stop identifying with your internal (potentially obsessive or self-critical) monologue and instead sense your true identity, which is unlimited and vast: the consciousness that exists everywhere and in every direction of time.

You can work with blue calcite to clear, activate, and align your throat chakra (the energy center that resides at your throat) to help you know your truth, speak your truth, and heal your relationship with your creativity and self-expression.

It's natural for your degree of joy to fluctuate, but if it's been a while since you've felt that expansive sense of connection and delight, blue calcite can help you tap right back into the frequency of joy.

Try running your calcite under cold water for a minute or two, drying it off with a clean towel, and then wearing it (in a pouch or as jewelry) near your throat. Place your hand over it. Close your eyes, breathe, and see if you can sense the healing, joy-filled energy coming from the stone. Then imagine that energy positively affecting you in precisely the way you desire.

Malachite

Malachite, with its elaborate green swirls, is a stone of divine alchemy. It helps bring about a perfect balance and synthesis of energies as it assists you in releasing that which no longer serves you while simultaneously magnetizing exactly what you need. This dynamic makes it an excellent stone for healing and bolstering the heart, improving your wealth vibration, and strengthening your physical health. Malachite can also be employed to help you hear your guides, ancestors, and angels, and to become even more attuned and committed to your unique spiritual path.

First, place your malachite outside on the earth for a minute or two (stone, grass, moss, or soil will all do). Then, hold it in your right hand. Sense or imagine the stone's alchemical emanation: the current of energy that affects precisely the changes that will be most beneficial for everyone concerned. Then see or sense that emanation moving into the physical body and aura in such a way that naturally and effortlessly calibrates your vibration until you can't help but manifest the positive changes you'd most like to experience. (Although you don't actually have to know exactly what this will look like. Just working with the intention "for my truest good" is enough. You can trust the details to the universe.)

Rutilated Quartz

This quartz filled with filaments of rutile is excellent for cutting away thought patterns and commitments that distract you from living your dreams and merrily flowing along your most ideal and inspired stream. It also helps energize you and balance your thoughts while guiding you to take effective action in the physical world. In other words, it helps you focus on your life path and manifest the truest desires of your heart.

Spread a small white cloth outside in bright sunlight and place your rutilated quartz on the cloth. Let it soak in the sun for a minute or two. Then use your finger to hold it to your third eye—the energy center at the center of your forehead, just above the center of your eyebrows. Close your eyes and concentrate your attention into the stone. Gently, lovingly, and with as much joyful expectation as you can muster, ask the stone to help you align your life with its most ideal flow and to concentrate on the activities that will help you live your dreams.

Selenite

Selenite is most often used as a cleansing stone: it absorbs and neutralizes stuck, heavy, frenetic, or otherwise wonky energy and leaves only the most positive and beneficial vibrations in its wake. You can wear it, carry it, place it in an environment, or wave it around a person, place, or object to remove anything that is not for your purest and truest good.

But first: cleanse and activate your selenite by placing it in bright sunlight outdoors for three to five minutes. Never get your selenite wet because it will slowly dissolve. As mentioned above, selenite absorbs challenging vibrations, so to keep its energy sparkly clean, I recommend repeating the outdoor sunlight cleanse periodically and keeping it in a sunny windowsill when not in use.

* * *

As always with crystal work, feel into which crystal to work with at any given time. You might notice a pull to work with a particular crystal just by reading about it and sensing your excitement soar, or you might encounter a stone in a store and love spending time with it so much that you just know it will be healing for you to have nearby. Your intuition, curiosity, and enthusiasm are your magical compasses that will unfailingly lead you to the ingredients and practices that will yield the most powerful results.

When the Magick Fails
by JD Walker

Life is filled with disappointments. We have great expectations of our careers, our family, our leaders, and our idols. These expectations aren't always met. Perhaps the biggest disappointment is when we have great expectations of ourselves and we fail to achieve whatever it is we are striving for. This is true in everyday life. It is also true in our spiritual life.

What are we to think when the magick fails? In this case, I'm speaking of magick in the broadest sense—everything from true magickal workings to spiritual development, from expectations of how things should have turned out following a working to appeals to deity, whatever deity or spiritual entity you are appealing to.

At the very least, bad or no results can make us doubt ourselves. In the worst case, this kind of outcome can make us doubt our faith. Before you sink too far into self-recrimination or throw in the cauldron on your faith, maybe it's time to take a step back for a little in-depth review.

Finding the Source of the Problem

Most often when we don't achieve our ends, the problem is a matter that needs a little tweaking. Occasionally, we need to do a deep dive on our concept of spirituality. Let's leave the questions about spirituality alone for a moment and focus on some of the practical things that can most easily be addressed.

Practical Challenges

Time

Perhaps the first excuse that comes to mind when we fail at whatever task is "I didn't have the time to do what I could/would/should have done!" That rarely works with the boss. It doesn't work in the spiritual realm either. Simple tasks in this realm can take as few as thirty minutes. More complex rituals may take a few hours or days. Shortcutting won't do. If you are working a seven-day spell, you have to work it every day. You can't skip a day . . . or two . . . or more. If the ritual for your deity or ancestor should take an hour, you can't rush it through in twenty minutes—what my mother used to call "a kiss and a promise."

I was once asked to explain to someone how to get her poinsettia, a plant she had nurtured for about a year, to return to a nice red color in time for the holidays. I explained she had to control the light exposure very carefully every day by exposing it to light for ten hours a day and setting it in a dark place like a closet for fourteen hours each day. A month or so later I saw her again and she was furious with me. She was certain I didn't know what I was talking about. After she calmed down, I started to ask her about her care routine. Soon it became clear she was not following the light regimen. Some days she gave the plant light for twelve or more hours at a stretch. One weekend she forgot and left it in the closet for three days. She failed because she didn't commit to the full task.

The point is if you aren't going to give your workings or ritual the full time required, you shouldn't be surprised when the results are poor.

Focus

This may be the hardest to tackle. We are often told to "be in the moment" to get all we should out of life. Be in the moment for that family gathering—not working on something from our job. Be in the moment as our child explains a new science project—not making up a grocery list for the next trip to the store.

Focus is key in rituals and spellwork too. Regardless of what you are working on, you must be seeing, smelling, and feeling that project from start to finish. That means going into the work fully prepared with all your materials at hand. Think out and mentally walk through what you will do prior to starting. Once you start, invest, invest, invest all your thoughts and efforts into what you are doing. This is a time when we must truly experience a "time outside time and a place outside place."

At the end of some of the best workings or rituals I have been a part of, I feel as though I have awakened from a dream. Maybe an hour or so has passed, but it has felt like I am only working a few minutes. This doesn't happen with every single ritual or working, but it is what we should be striving for.

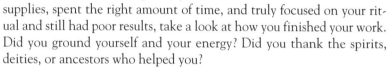

A Strong Finish

If you have taken care to gather your supplies, spent the right amount of time, and truly focused on your ritual and still had poor results, take a look at how you finished your work. Did you ground yourself and your energy? Did you thank the spirits, deities, or ancestors who helped you?

Did you do what was required at the end of the spell? If the working requires that you bury some part of the materials used, that means dig a hole and cover the stuff with soil. You don't have to dig to the other side of the world, but full contact with earth is required. You can't throw it in the trash or toss it out the car window. If the spell requires going to a crossroads, go to a crossroads. If it requires casting the material to the wind or into running water, find a safe place to do so.

I am sometimes asked for a common spell to get rid of a bothersome person. It requires a simple ritual that results in a powder that must then be put in someone's shoes or clothing pockets. When it fails, the problem is usually that the powder didn't get into the shoes or pockets. The user didn't think that part was important or was afraid the person would notice. In either case, the spell didn't fail—the practitioner did. The spell must be completed as directed if for no other reason than to honor the spell. This will also prove the practitioner's courage of conviction.

Spiritual Challenges

Realistic Expectations

How many times have I had someone ask me for a spell that would make them invisible or turn them into a wolf or other creature? How many times have I been asked for a working that will bring back a dear loved one when it is their time to go? More times than I care to remember.

The universe isn't a PEZ dispenser. You can't push a button and get a piece of metaphysical candy. Forget the popular fictional magic in

books, films, and games. True magick works, but it must follow the rules of nature—what we tend to call today the laws of physics. Yes, you can enhance your prospects of career advancement, but no, you can't be made company CEO overnight. Yes, you can make yourself more attractive to a prospective companion, but no, you can't force the latest celebrity to find you and fall madly in love with you.

Consider what you are asking. Does it break the laws of nature? Does it take away someone else's free will or divert them from their own personal destiny? Is this something you truly need or just something you want? Be honest with yourself before you act. This can save you a lot of heartache and wasted time.

Hit-and-Miss Dedication

I have experienced this problem in my own life. If I get slack in my daily devotions and regular seasonal observations, my spellwork suffers. My prayers to deity seem to go unnoticed. Why should this be any surprise? If we don't exercise our spiritual muscles, they atrophy just like regular muscles. If we don't keep the lines of communication open to friends and family, can we really expect them to be there for us in our time of need? We sometimes treat deity like a doting grandparent who waits anxiously by the phone for our text or call. Humans are not the center of the universe. However, regardless of your tradition, if you stay in touch through regular prayers and observations, you will likely see a better response in those times of need.

Here's another suggestion. Renew your spiritual studies. You aren't the same person you were when you first stepped on this spiritual path. Give yourself time and room to grow beyond what you always did in the past. This proves dedication and a commitment to that path.

Living in This World

Are you spending too much time asking for things from the spiritual realm that you could realistically accomplish in the everyday world? If you want more money, work for it. Ask for a raise. Look for a better-paying job. If you want a companion, go to those places where the kind of person you want to meet likely hangs out. Put yourself out there in new situations. Before you crack open the Book of Shadows, take some time to figure out what you are asking for. Then ask yourself how you can attain it without magick. If you still need to do a little hocus-pocus, a little appeal to the ancestors, the extra effort you put out in the real world can only enhance your magick.

Conclusion

Frequently, when we complain to our peers about our failures, we'll hear them say, "Well, if it didn't work out the way you expected, maybe the universe is telling you that you don't need it. It's protecting you from a bad outcome."

This response is rarely what we want to hear, and frankly, it's a bit of a cop-out. As Pagans, we are generally told that the universe can be manipulated to our ends with the right approach. Hearing someone tell us the universe doesn't have to cooperate is a bit like saying Big Brother is watching and he knows better than you what you need.

This isn't to say we don't ask for stupid outcomes. We do. We all do. If the universe doesn't respond in the way you expected after due diligence, you might need to seek guidance from a reader or counselor you trust to see what might be holding you back. You could cast the cards, runes, or bones yourself, but generally, we have a blind eye when it comes to our own desires. Whatever you do, spend some time with yourself to better understand what you are searching for.

Above all, keep the faith. We all struggle. We all get disillusioned. However, if you look closely at your faith, you will see that tiny spark that drew you here in the first place. Embrace it. Nurture it. Develop it. Let it envelop you for better outcomes in the future.

January 2024

S	M	T	W
	1 New Year's Day Mercury Direct	2	◑
7	8	9	10
14	15 Martin Luther King Jr. Day	16	◐
21	22	23	24
28	29	30	31
4	5	6	7

T	F	S	Notes
4	5	6	
☽	12	13	
18	19	20 Sun enters Aquarius	
☺ Cold Moon	26	27	
1	2	3	
8	9	10	

29

January

1 Monday
3rd ♍
☿ D 10:08 pm
Color: Silver

2 Tuesday
3rd ♍
☽ v/c 6:36 pm
☽ enters ♎ 7:47 pm
Color: Gray

◑ Wednesday
3rd ♎
4th quarter 10:30 pm
Color: White

Laha is the Gaulish goddess of springs and wells.

4 Thursday
4th ♎
♂ enters ♑ 9:58 am
Color: Turquoise

5 Friday
4th ♎
☽ v/c 6:41 am
☽ enters ♏ 7:39 am
Color: Purple

Parsnip Tea Bread

½ cup dried cranberries
½ cup apple cider, warmed
¾ cup oat flour
¾ cup flour
1 tsp. baking powder
½ tsp. baking soda
½ tsp. salt
1 tsp. cinnamon
¼ tsp. ginger
½ cup brown sugar, packed
2 eggs
¾ cup olive oil
½ cup honey
1 tsp. vanilla extract
2 cups finely grated parsnip

Preheat oven to 350°F. Butter a loaf pan. Soak the cranberries in the cider for 30 minutes. In a mixing bowl, stir together the flours, baking powder, baking soda, salt, cinnamon, and ginger. Make a well in the center and add the brown sugar, eggs, oil, honey, and vanilla. Mix together to combine. Drain the cranberries and stir into the batter with the parsnip. Scrape the batter into the loaf pan and bake for 50 minutes, or until a wooden pick comes out clean. Let cool, then run a knife along the sides of the pan to loosen.

—Laurel Woodward

6 Saturday

4th ♏
Color: Blue

7 Sunday

4th ♏
☽ v/c 3:22 pm
☽ enters ♐ 4:08 pm
Color: Yellow

The bodhi tree, a type of fig, teaches enlightenment.

January

8 Monday
4th ♐
Color: White

9 Tuesday
4th ♐
☽ v/c 1:24 pm
☽ enters ♑ 8:33 pm
Color: Red

For abundance, wear agate.

10 Wednesday
4th ♑
Color: Topaz

☽ Thursday
4th ♑
New Moon 6:57 am
☽ v/c 9:33 pm
☽ enters ♒ 10:01 pm
Color: Green

Mars direct

12 Friday
1st ♒
Color: Pink

*Pink is empathetic and good
for healing emotional injuries.*

Set in Eastern Standard Time (EST)

13 Saturday

1st ♒

☽ v/c 4:59 am
☿ enters ♑ 9:49 pm
☽ enters ♓ 10:29 pm
Color: Brown

*Hares are related to fecundity, the Moon,
and the many goddesses in charge of those.*

14 Sunday

1st ♓
Color: Gold

15 Monday

1st ♓

☽ v/c 11:33 pm

☽ enters ♈ 11:49 pm

Color: Gray

Martin Luther King Jr. Day

16 Tuesday

1st ♈

Color: Black

◐ Wednesday

1st ♈

2nd quarter 10:53 pm

Color: Yellow

The Pythia washed in the Castalian
Spring before giving prophecies.

18 Thursday

2nd ♈

☽ v/c 3:03 am

☽ enters ♉ 3:12 am

Color: White

19 Friday

2nd ♉

Color: Rose

Abigail Hobbs

Abigail Hobbs of Salem Village was arrested on April 18, 1692, on charges of Witchcraft. Hobbs, who is believed to have been between the ages of fourteen and sixteen at the time, was noted as being quite rebellious. It was said that she would wander into the woods late at night, boasting to others that she was unafraid because she had sold her body and soul to the "old boy."

Hobbs confessed that she had met the Devil in the woods several years prior, at which time he promised her fine things if she would become a Witch. She went on to claim that she tormented others by sticking poppets with pins and thorns, all of which had been given to her by another accused Witch, George Burroughs. Additionally, Hobbs admitted to attending a gathering of Witches that took place in the Reverend Samuel Parris's pasture, during which they feasted on red bread and wine.

Although a warrant had been signed for Hobbs's execution, she was given a reprieve in January 1693.

—Kelden

20 Saturday
2nd ♉
☽ v/c 8:57 am
☽ enters ♊ 8:58 am
☉ enters ♒ 9:07 am
♀ enters ♒ 7:50 pm
Color: Indigo

Sun enters Aquarius

21 Sunday
2nd ♊
Color: Orange

Celtic Tree Month of Rowan begins

22 Monday
2nd ♊
☽ v/c 3:40 pm
☽ enters ♋ 4:51 pm
Color: Silver

23 Tuesday

2nd ♋
♀ enters ♑ 3:50 am
Color: Maroon

*Blackbirds are associated with
water, intuition, and inspiration.*

24 Wednesday

2nd ♋
☽ v/c 5:58 pm
Color: White

☺ Thursday
2nd ♋
☽ enters ♌ 2:37 am
Full Moon 12:54 pm
Color: Crimson

Cold Moon

26 Friday

3rd ♌
☽ v/c 4:19 pm
Color: Coral

*Singing bowls resonate when rubbed around
the rim and are often used in meditation.*

January Moon of Dreaming

We walk in a dream through the darkened landscape January offers and doubt that spring will ever come. For how can anything survive winter's cruel hand? But the murmurs of transformation are truly at play deep within our Mother's womb. And if we close our eyes and listen, we can perceive the signs. Patience is required of us. Take a breath and dream.

We look to the Full Moon of January and dream of things that can be as we face the cold and darkness in our own lives. We must trust that transformation is at hand. Make yourself a cup of herbal tea and light a candle. Write down those dreams that lie sleeping just under the surface. This is your first step in your journey.

—Monica Crosson

27 Saturday

3rd ♌
♅ D 2:35 am
☽ enters ♍ 2:11 pm
Color: Gray

In Zapotec lore, Cocijo is the god
of lightning and unpleasant weather.

28 Sunday

3rd ♍
Color: Amber

February 2024

S	M	T	W
4	5	6	7
11	12	13	14 Valentine's Day
18 Sun enters Pisces	19 Presidents' Day	20	21
25	26	27	28
3	4	5	6

T	F	S	Notes
1	◑ 3		
	Imbolc Groundhog Day		
8	☽	10	
		Lunar New Year (Dragon)	
15	◐	17	
22	23	☺	
		Quickening Moon	
29	1	2	
7	8	9	

29 Monday
3rd ♍
☽ v/c 6:20 pm
Color: Lavender

Solomon's seal is used as an offertory incense.

30 Tuesday
3rd ♍
☽ enters ♎ 3:04 am
Color: Scarlet

31 Wednesday
3rd ♎
Color: Brown

1 Thursday
3rd ♎
☽ v/c 4:03 am
☽ enters ♏ 3:37 pm
Color: Purple

*Plumeria attracts favorable
attention and empowers persuasion.*

◑ Friday
3rd ♏
4th quarter 6:18 pm
Color: White

Imbolc
Groundhog Day

Imbolc: The Signs

At Imbolc, the halfway point between Yule and Ostara, many regions are still in the grip of the snow and cold. But all around us are the signs that the season is beginning to change.

Daylight hours lengthen. From the still-frozen earth, crocuses nudge their way through the snow. Some signs, however, can't be seen. From the roots, sap unseen and silent rises to renew the vitality of every tree. Even the twilight of early evening begins to show signs of change. Dusk lingers. Darkness doesn't fall as suddenly as it did a month ago. Now the dusk has a soft, leisurely glow.

Mark this sabbat by honoring the signs of nature's changes. Upon your altar place a package of seeds. Meditate on how something as small as a seed will bring forth the sign of a changing season and the power of the life force renewed. If you don't have a garden, do this meditation by using a small new houseplant. Tend it and think of nature's changing signs as it grows.

It may still snow, but the signs at Imbolc tell us the life force of Earth is eternal.

—James Kambos

---

3 Saturday

4th ♏
☽ v/c 10:24 pm
Color: Black

---

4 Sunday

4th ♏
☽ enters ♐ 1:28 am
Color: Gold

Imbolc cross-quarter day
(Sun reaches 15° Aquarius)

February

5 Monday
4th ♐
☿ enters ♒ 12:10 am
Color: Ivory

6 Tuesday
4th ♐
☽ v/c 12:06 am
☽ enters ♑ 7:08 am
Color: White

*The color white clears away old
energy to make way for the new.*

7 Wednesday
4th ♑
Color: Yellow

*Nightshade is sacred to Atropos, one of the
three Fates who cuts the thread of life.*

8 Thursday
4th ♑
☽ v/c 2:52 am
☽ enters ♒ 8:59 am
Color: Green

☽ Friday
4th ♒
☽ v/c 5:59 pm
New Moon 5:59 pm
Color: Rose

Raccoons are all about resourcefulness.

10 Saturday

1st ≈≈

☽ enters ♓ 8:42 am

Color: Gray

Lunar New Year (Dragon)

11 Sunday

1st ♓

Color: Yellow

February

12 Monday
1st ♓
☽ v/c 7:32 am
☽ enters ♈ 8:26 am
Color: Silver

13 Tuesday
1st ♈
♂ enters ♒ 1:05 am
Color: Black

Mardi Gras (Fat Tuesday)

14 Wednesday

1st ♈
☽ v/c 5:21 am
☽ enters ♉ 10:02 am
Color: Topaz

Valentine's Day
Ash Wednesday

15 Thursday

1st ♉
Color: White

Friday

1st ♉
☽ v/c 10:01 am
2nd quarter 10:01 am
♀ enters ♒ 11:05 am
☽ enters ♊ 2:39 pm
Color: Purple

The Navajo honor the springs and wells around Black Mesa.

Set in Eastern Standard Time (EST)

White Bean Soup

2 cups dried white beans, rinsed,
    sorted, and soaked overnight
4 pieces of bacon, chopped (optional,
    or substitute 2 T. butter)
1½ cups chopped onion
½ cup chopped carrot
½ cup chopped celery
4 cups chicken or vegetable broth
1 cup water
1 tsp. herbes de Provence

Drain your beans, rinse, and set aside. In a large stockpot, cook bacon for 4 minutes. Stir in onion and cook until onion pieces turn clear. Stir in the carrot and celery and cook 3 more minutes. Add the beans, broth, and water and bring to a boil. Stir in the herbes de Provence and reduce heat to a simmer. Loosely cover the pot so that the steam can vent as it simmers. Cook for 90 minutes or until the beans are tender. Keep an eye on the liquid and add a cup of water or broth if needed. Serve hot with a hunk of rustic bread for a warm and satisfying meal. Makes 4 to 6 servings.

    White beans such as cannellini, lima, and navy beans are often combined in recipes and used to support intentions to aid communication, inspire inspiration, and draw luck and prosperity.

—Laurel Woodward

17 Saturday
2nd ♊
Color: Indigo

18 Sunday
2nd ♊
☽ v/c 10:21 pm
☽ enters ♋ 10:25 pm
☉ enters ♓ 11:13 pm
Color: Orange

Sun enters Pisces
Celtic Tree Month of Ash begins

February

19 Monday
2nd ♋
Color: Gray

Presidents' Day

20 Tuesday
2nd ♋
Color: Maroon

Embrace personal power with rhododendron.

21 Wednesday
2nd ♋
☽ v/c 1:38 am
☽ enters ♌ 8:40 am
Color: White

22 Thursday
2nd ♌
☽ v/c 11:18 pm
Color: Crimson

For knowledge of death and the hereafter, turn to vultures.

23 Friday
2nd ♌
☿ enters ♓ 2:29 am
☽ enters ♍ 8:38 pm
Color: Coral

February Moon of Quickening

The starkness of winter allows us to reevaluate our intentions. Like the trees bereft of leaves, we may feel exposed and vulnerable. But instead of ducking away to the safety of our tidy corners, look upon those bare bones and ask yourself, "How can I better support myself throughout the upcoming year?" The signs are all around us that the earth is preparing to awaken. Are you?

Under the Full Moon in February, feel the quickening deep within your spirit and prepare yourself for your awakening. This is not a time of timidity: stand with arms outstretched under the Moon's pallid glow, cry into the darkness your intentions, and feel the earth under your feet respond in kind.

—Monica Crosson

☺ **Saturday**
2nd ♍
Full Moon 7:30 am
Color: Blue

25 Sunday
3rd ♍
Color: Yellow

March 2024

S	M	T	W
◐	4	5	6
☽ Daylight Saving Time begins at 2 am	11	12	13
◑ St. Patrick's Day	18	19 Ostara / Spring Equinox Sun enters Aries	20
24	☻ Storm Moon Lunar Eclipse	26	27
31	1	2	3

T	F	S	Notes
	1	2	
7	8	9	
14	15	16	
21	22	23	
28	29	30	
4	5	6	

February/March

26 Monday
3rd ♍
☽ v/c 2:35 am
☽ enters ♎ 9:29 am
Color: White

For insight, try moldavite.

27 Tuesday
3rd ♎
☽ v/c 1:22 pm
Color: Scarlet

28 Wednesday
3rd ♎
☽ enters ♏ 10:09 pm
Color: Brown

Vervain is known as the enchanter's herb.

29 Thursday
3rd ♏
Color: Purple

Leap Day

1 Friday
3rd ♏
Color: White

Set in Eastern Standard Time (EST)

Jeanne Boisdeau

Executed for sorcery in 1594, French woman Jeanne Boisdeau confessed that she and other Witches from all over the country gathered on Midsummer night. She explained that these Sabbath meetings took place atop Puy de Dôme, a lava dome in central France. It was noted that in order to get there, the Witches would mount their broomsticks and be carried off by the wind.

Boisdeau explained that on Puy de Dôme the Witches gathered in a circle, in the center of which the Devil appeared as a he-goat. The members of the coven each lit a candle from the black one their Master wore between his horns. After this, the Devil said Mass, using a slice of radish in place of the sacrament. Boisdeau went on to say that the Devil gave the Witches various charms as well as the ability to predict the future.

Finally, Jeanne claimed that the Witches danced in a ring with their faces outward. During this dance, they all held hands, while the eldest Witch held on to the Devil's tail.

—Kelden

---

2 Saturday

3rd ♏
☽ v/c 2:47 am
☽ enters ♐ 8:56 am
Color: Black

To remember past lives, use hollyhock.

◑ Sunday

3rd ♐
4th quarter 10:23 am
Color: Gold

March

4 Monday

4th ♐
☽ v/c 10:41 am
☽ enters ♑ 4:15 pm
Color: Ivory

*Aspen forms vast stands of stems from a clonal
colony, making it a great symbol of community.*

5 Tuesday

4th ♑
Color: Red

6 Wednesday

4th ♑
☽ v/c 2:35 pm
☽ enters ♒ 7:38 pm
Color: White

7 Thursday

4th ♒
Color: Turquoise

Stringed instruments relate to the element of water.

8 Friday

4th ♒
☽ v/c 1:56 pm
☽ enters ♓ 8:03 pm
Color: Pink

Mushroom and Blue Cheese Quiche

1 unbaked piecrust
8 oz. mushrooms (crimini and oyster
   work well)
2 T. butter
1 clove garlic, minced
2–3 T. chopped shallots
¼ cup crumbled blue cheese
6 eggs
1 cup heavy cream
½ cup parmesan
Salt and pepper to taste

Preheat oven to 375°F. Line a deep-dish pie pan with the piecrust and set aside. If you don't have a deep-dish pan, use a standard pie pan with a baking sheet under it during baking. Wash the mushrooms and pat them dry. Separate the caps from the stalks. Slice the caps and dice the stalks. In a saucepan, melt the butter. Add the mushrooms and cook for 4 minutes, stirring often, until browned. Add the garlic and shallots and cook 3 more minutes. Scrape the mixture into the piecrust and top with the blue cheese. Set aside. In a mixing bowl, beat together the eggs, cream, and parmesan. Pour over mushroom mixture. Bake 40 to 45 minutes, or until the quiche looks puffed and firm. Serve hot and season with salt and pepper to taste.

—Laurel Woodward

9 Saturday

4th ♓
☿ enters ♈ 11:03 pm
Color: Gray

☽ Sunday

4th ♓
New Moon 5:00 am
☽ v/c 3:45 pm
☽ enters ♈ 8:19 pm
Color: Amber

Ramadan begins at sundown
Daylight Saving Time begins at 2 am

March

11 Monday
1st ♈
♀ enters ♓ 5:50 pm
Color: Lavender

Vodou calls on Baron Samedi as Gentleman Death.

12 Tuesday
1st ♈
☽ v/c 7:08 am
☽ enters ♉ 8:28 pm
Color: Gray

Linden is a popular ward tree. Its flowers make excellent honey.

13 Wednesday
1st ♉
Color: Yellow

14 Thursday
1st ♉
☽ v/c 6:29 pm
☽ enters ♊ 11:16 pm
Color: White

15 Friday
1st ♊
Color: Purple

Wear smoky quartz in mourning.

16 Saturday

1st ♊
Color: Blue

◑ Sunday

1st ♊
2nd quarter 12:11 am
☽ v/c 12:43 am
☽ enters ♋ 5:40 am
Color: Yellow

March

18 Monday

2nd ♋
Color: Silver

Celtic Tree Month of Alder begins

19 Tuesday

2nd ♋
☽ v/c 2:52 pm
☽ enters ♌ 3:33 pm
☉ enters ♈ 11:06 pm
Color: Scarlet

Ostara/Spring Equinox
International Astrology Day
Sun enters Aries

20 Wednesday

2nd ♌
Color: Brown

21 Thursday

2nd ♌
Color: Purple

Dragon's blood incense amplifies rituals and spells.

22 Friday

2nd ♌
☽ v/c 2:34 am
☽ enters ♍ 3:42 am
♂ enters ♓ 7:47 pm
Color: Coral

Set in Eastern Daylight Time (EDT)

Ostara: The Promise

Ostara, the vernal equinox, is a celebration of rebirth and renewal. It's the promise of life eternal. The green world holds the promise of rebirth. The grass greens and a veil of green mists the trees. Daffodil foliage pierces the soil, greeting the spring Sun. In the early evening the small *Hylas*, or "peepers," can be heard singing their spring song from the swampy margins. It's a song as ancient as time itself. It's the voice of renewal and enduring life.

To observe Ostara's promise of life's eternal cycle, you'll need two hard-boiled eggs. Place them on your altar. Hold one egg. Think of how it holds the promise of new life. Peel the egg and discard the shell. Slowly, with purpose, eat the egg. The white represents the future. The yolk symbolizes the life-giving Sun. Last, decorate the second egg with a life-affirming design of your choice. Flowers, a cross, and a pentacle are a few ideas. Keep this egg for a while, then discard it.

Let Ostara's promise of new life spark your energy and creativity.

—James Kambos

23 Saturday
2nd ♍
Color: Indigo

Purim begins at sundown

24 Sunday
2nd ♍
☽ v/c 11:49 am
☽ enters ♎ 4:37 pm
Color: Gold

Palm Sunday

March

☺ Monday
2nd ♎
Full Moon 3:00 am
Color: Gray

Storm Moon
Lunar Eclipse, 3:00 am, 5° ♎ 07'

26 Tuesday
3rd ♎
☽ v/c 7:09 pm
Color: Black

27 Wednesday
3rd ♎
☽ enters ♏ 5:03 am
Color: White

28 Thursday
3rd ♏
Color: Green

Use green to promote growth and fertility.

29 Friday
3rd ♏
☽ v/c 11:40 am
☽ enters ♐ 3:52 pm
Color: Rose

Good Friday

March Moon of Awakening

March is a fickle month. One day, the world feels anew. The very air is tinged with the promise of green that lulls us into a false sense of spring's arrival, only to be sent retreating to the warmth of our fires the next day when winter's cruel breath makes a sudden return.

We are the same—one day, enthusiastic and confident in our ability to take on the world, only to feel enveloped by doubt and hesitation the next day. Be kind to yourself if this happens, as awakenings are not an easy thing.

March's Full Moon asks us to tend the roots of our soul with tenderness. Too much too soon can disturb our growth. Plant seeds as ritual to remind yourself that all good happens at its own pace.

—Monica Crosson

---

30 Saturday

3rd ♐
Color: Brown

For courage and strength, use lion imagery.

---

31 Sunday

3rd ♐
☽ v/c 8:16 pm
Color: Orange

Easter

April 2024

S	M	T	W
	◐ 1 All Fools' Day Mercury Retrograde	2	3
7	🌙 8 Solar Eclipse	9	10
14	◑ 15	16	17
21	22 Earth Day	😊 23 Wind Moon	24
28	29	30	1
5	6	7	8

T	F	S	Notes
4	5	6	
11	12	13	
18	19 Sun enters Taurus	20	
25 Mercury Direct	26	27	
2	3	4	
9	10	11	

April

◑ Monday

3rd ♐
☽ enters ♑ 12:05 am
☿ ℞ 6:14 pm
4th quarter 11:15 pm
Color: White

All Fools' Day
April Fools' Day
Mercury retrograde until April 25

2 Tuesday

4th ♑
Color: Gray

*The Ganges is a sacred river in India and
has been granted legal rights of personhood.*

3 Wednesday

4th ♑
☽ v/c 1:40 am
☽ enters ♒ 5:08 am
Color: Topaz

4 Thursday

4th ♒
Color: Crimson

5 Friday

4th ♒
♀ enters ♈ 12:00 am
☽ v/c 1:40 am
☽ enters ♓ 7:13 am
Color: Purple

Individual Spinach Soufflés

1½ T. butter, plus more for the pans
⅓ cup grated parmesan, divided
1½ T. flour
⅔ cup milk
½ lb. fresh spinach, blanched, drained,
　and chopped
Salt and pepper to taste
1 T. lemon juice
¼ tsp. nutmeg
6 eggs, separated, discarding 1 yolk or
　reusing for a different dish
½ cup grated cheddar cheese

Preheat oven to 375°F. Generously butter a muffin tin or 6 4-ounce rame-kins. Sprinkle parmesan into the bottom of each. In a saucepan, melt the butter. Add the flour and stir to make a roux. Cook, stirring constantly, for 2 minutes. Stir in milk and cook for 1 minute. Turn off heat and stir in spinach, salt, pepper, lemon juice, and nutmeg. Stir egg yolks and cheese into the hot mixture. In a mixing bowl, beat the egg whites with a pinch of salt until stiff. Fold the egg whites into the spinach mixture. Divide the mixture between the ramekins and bake for 20 minutes. Makes 6 servings.

—Laurel Woodward

6 Saturday
4th ♓
Color: Indigo

Chickadees bring happiness and adaptability.

7 Sunday
4th ♓
☽ v/c 4:27 am
☽ enters ♈ 7:25 am
Color: Yellow

April

 Monday
4th ♈
New Moon 2:21 pm
☽ v/c 10:39 pm
Color: Gray

Solar Eclipse, 2:21 pm, 19° ♈ 24'

9 Tuesday
1st ♈
☽ enters ♉ 7:23 am
Color: White

Ramadan ends

10 Wednesday
1st ♉
Color: Brown

11 Thursday
1st ♉
☽ v/c 6:04 am
☽ enters ♊ 8:59 am
Color: Turquoise

For divination and wishes, use dandelion.

12 Friday
1st ♊
Color: Rose

Set in Eastern Daylight Time (EDT)

Florence Newton

On March 24, 1661, Florence Newton of Youghal, Ireland, was arrested on charges of Witchcraft.

During her trial, Newton's main accuser was a maid named Mary Langdon. According to Langdon, she became violently ill—including vomiting pins and needles—after Newton had kissed her. Days after this incident, she claimed that Newton and a man clothed in silk appeared at her bedside. The man asked that she promise to follow his advice and in turn she would have whatever her heart desired. Langdon piously rejected this offer and shortly thereafter became ill.

Another of Newton's accusers was the widow of one of her prison guards, David Jones. The widow testified that Newton had managed to kiss her late husband's hand through a prison grate. Subsequently, Jones fell ill with a great pain in his arm and heart. After fourteen days, during which time the man repeatedly cried out against Newton, he died.

The final verdict of Newton's case is missing from historical records, but it remains likely that she was found guilty and executed.

—Kelden

13 Saturday
1st ♊
☽ v/c 10:46 am
☽ enters ♋ 1:45 pm
Color: Black

14 Sunday
1st ♋
Color: Amber

Hattic mythology upholds Inara as the goddess of protection, mainly of animals.

April

 Monday

1st ♋
2nd quarter 3:13 pm
☽ v/c 7:22 pm
☽ enters ♌ 10:24 pm
Color: Lavender

Celtic Tree Month of Willow begins

16 Tuesday

2nd ♌
Color: Maroon

Danger can be warded off with tiger's eye.

17 Wednesday

2nd ♌
Color: Yellow

18 Thursday

2nd ♌
☽ v/c 8:02 am
☽ enters ♍ 10:10 am
Color: Purple

Otters are playful but can assist in travel between
worlds because they live in water and earth.

19 Friday

2nd ♍
☉ enters ♉ 10:00 am
Color: White

Sun enters Taurus

20 Saturday

2nd ♍
☽ v/c 8:20 pm
☽ enters ♎ 11:08 pm
Color: Gray

For authenticity and decision-making, use camellia.

21 Sunday

2nd ♎
Color: Gold

April

22 Monday

2nd ♎
☽ v/c 7:24 pm
Color: Silver

Passover begins at sundown
Earth Day

☺ Tuesday

2nd ♎
☽ enters ♏ 11:20 am
Full Moon 7:49 pm
Color: Black

Wind Moon

24 Wednesday

3rd ♏
Color: White

25 Thursday

3rd ♏
☿ D 8:54 am
☽ v/c 7:17 pm
☽ enters ♐ 9:37 pm
Color: Green

Meercury direct

26 Friday

3rd ♐
Color: Pink

April Moon of Rebirth

Regeneration is at hand as once again the landscape unfurls around us. Fresh and full of promise, April feels like youth. Take advantage of this energy and use it to fuel your own transformation. Remember, sacred is the new beginning and sacred is our journey within this world. It is up to us to set our own pace.

Under April's Full Moon, we acknowledge a world anew and our place in it. We are courageous as we take on needed change and embrace the growth that accompanies it. Celebrate rebirth with a ritual bath scented with bright citrusy essential oils, and use a salt scrub to wash away the layers of old thinking. Arise with the knowledge that anything is possible.

—Monica Crosson

27 Saturday
3rd ♐
Color: Brown

Use brown for animal magic.

28 Sunday
3rd ♐
☽ v/c 3:31 am
☽ enters ♑ 5:37 am
Color: Amber

Nile lotus incense promotes enlightenment and suits Egyptian practices.

May 2024

S	M	T	W
			◑ Beltane
5	6	☽	8
12 Mother's Day	13	14	◑
19	20 Sun enters Gemini	21	22
26	27 Memorial Day	28	29
2	3	4	5

T	F	S	Notes
2	3	4	
9	10	11	
16	17	18	
☺ Flower Moon	24	25	
◑	31	1	
6	7	8	

April/May

29 Monday

3rd ♑
♀ enters ♉ 7:31 am
Color: Gray

Carry myrtle leaves to attract love and friendship.

30 Tuesday

3rd ♑
☽ v/c 11:19 am
☽ enters ♒ 11:20 am
♂ enters ♈ 11:33 am
Color: Red

Passover ends

◖ Wednesday

3rd ♒
4th quarter 7:27 am
Color: Yellow

Beltane/May Day

2 Thursday

4th ♒
☽ v/c 5:28 am
♀ ℞ 1:46 pm
☽ enters ♓ 2:52 pm
Color: Purple

3 Friday

4th ♓
Color: Coral

Orthodox Good Friday

Beltane: The Return

At Beltane we honor and celebrate the union of the God and Goddess. From this union the earth is blessed with the return of abundance. It can be seen and heard all around us. The seeds sprout and trees signal the return by once again spreading a leafy canopy. The birds know it. They sing their dawn chorus just as they have done for thousands of years.

In rural areas farmers return to the fields, turning the earth, the soil rising in rich dark brown waves. Soon, the earth will return their efforts by bringing forth crops to feed and sustain us.

To honor the natural world at Beltane we need to get close to nature. As you think about the union of the Goddess and God, go outside if possible. Walk with nature. Really look at, and really see, the beauty in a blade of grass, the wild violets, and the shiny new leaves. You can do this in a city park or your yard. Buy a bouquet of flowers. Display them on your altar as a tribute to nature's return.

—James Kambos

4 Saturday

4th ♓
☽ v/c 3:06 pm
☽ enters ♈ 4:41 pm
Color: Blue

Beltane cross-quarter day (Sun reaches 15° Taurus)

5 Sunday

4th ♈
Color: Orange

Cinco de Mayo
Orthodox Easter

May

6 Monday

4th ♈
☽ v/c 1:57 am
☽ enters ♉ 5:42 pm
Color: Ivory

☽ Tuesday
4th ♉
New Moon 11:22 pm
Color: Gray

*A guiro, or croaker, often carved to resemble a frog, has
notches that make a ribbet sound when stroked with a stick.*

8 Wednesday

1st ♉
☽ v/c 5:55 pm
☽ enters ♊ 7:20 pm
Color: White

9 Thursday
1st ♊
Color: Crimson

*The Australian Aboriginal lizard men Wati-kutjara descended the
mountains during the Dreaming and journeyed across the desert.*

10 Friday
1st ♊
☽ v/c 9:49 pm
☽ enters ♋ 11:13 pm
Color: Pink

Rowan belongs to the rose family and wards against evil spirits.

Set in Eastern Daylight Time (EDT)

11 Saturday

1st ♋
Color: Brown

12 Sunday

1st ♋
Color: Gold

Mother's Day

13 Monday

1st ♋
☽ v/c 5:13 am
☽ enters ♌ 6:36 am
Color: White

Celtic Tree Month of Hawthorn begins

14 Tuesday

1st ♌
Color: Scarlet

Lodestones attract luck.

◐ Wednesday

1st ♌
2nd quarter 7:48 am
☽ v/c 12:41 pm
☿ enters ♉ 1:05 pm
☽ enters ♍ 5:33 pm
Color: Brown

16 Thursday

2nd ♍
Color: Turquoise

Carry quince seeds to protect against physical attacks.

17 Friday

2nd ♍
Color: Rose

Focaccia

3 cups bread flour
½ tsp. salt
½ tsp. sugar
1½ tsp. instant or rapid-rise yeast
1 cup warm water
2 T. olive oil

In a mixing bowl, stir together flour, salt, sugar, and yeast. Stir in the water and olive oil until a raggedy dough forms and no dry flour remains. Dump the dough onto a lightly floured work surface and knead, working the dough until it becomes smooth and elastic, about 10 minutes. If the dough is too dry, sprinkle it with water as you knead. If it is sticky, sprinkle it with flour. Transfer dough to oiled bowl, cover the bowl with oiled plastic wrap, and let rest until doubled, about 1 or 2 hours. Roll the dough into a ball and set it on a baking sheet. Press it to make a 10-inch disk and cover with oiled plastic wrap. Let rise for 30 minutes. Then take your finger and press into the dough to cover the top with depressions. Cover dough and let it rise for 30 minutes. Preheat oven to 400°F.

I recommend topping the dough with sautéed onion, a drizzle of olive oil, and a sprinkle of salt. Bake for 25 minutes.

—Laurel Woodward

18 Saturday
2nd ♍
☽ v/c 5:09 am
☽ enters ♎ 6:23 am
Color: Gray

19 Sunday
2nd ♎
☽ v/c 11:48 am
Color: Amber

Porcupines deal in respect and protection. Their arsenal makes them very phlegmatic creatures.

May

20 Monday

2nd ♎︎
☉ enters ♊︎ 8:59 am
☽ enters ♏︎ 6:34 pm
Color: Gray

Victoria Day (Canada)
Sun enters Gemini

21 Tuesday

2nd ♏︎
Color: Red

22 Wednesday

2nd ♏︎
Color: Topaz

*Fast luck incense works for money, love, or business
and makes a good choice for a magical emergency kit.*

☺ Thursday

2nd ♏︎
☽ v/c 3:28 am
☽ enters ♐︎ 4:24 am
Full Moon 9:53 am
♀ enters ♊︎ 4:30 pm
Color: White

Flower Moon

24 Friday

3rd ♐︎
Color: Coral

May Moon of Mirth

The season of green is upon us. During this time of light and laughter, when merriment is the order of the day, we dance our circles without a care in the world. The air is tinged with the scent of honeysuckle, and the songs of the Fae can be heard just beyond the drone of insects, who dip among the hawthorn flowers. The earth is fertile and in celebration—why not go into the greenwood with someone special for a springtime tryst?

Under May's joyous Full Moon, practice your ritual skyclad and experience the exquisite sensation of moonglow on your skin. This is a time to celebrate the earth's fertility with music, dance, and sensuality. Let your hair down and enjoy the raucous energy as we enter the light half of the year.

—Monica Crosson

---

25 Saturday

3rd ♐
☽ v/c 10:47 am
☽ enters ♑ 11:36 am
♃ enters ♊ 7:15 pm
Color: Black

---

26 Sunday

3rd ♑
Color: Orange

Plant oak trees for protection. They also host the largest number of wildlife species in many bioregions.

June 2024

S	M	T	W
2	3	4	5
9	10	11	12
16 Father's Day	17	18	19
23	24	25	26
30	1	2	3

T	F	S	Notes
		1	
☽	7	8	
13	◐	15	
	Flag Day		
20	☺	22	
Litha / Summer Solstice Sun enters Cancer	Strong Sun Moon		
27	◑	29	
4	5	6	

27 Monday

3rd ♑
☽ v/c 4:02 pm
☽ enters ♒ 4:45 pm
Color: Ivory

Memorial Day

28 Tuesday

3rd ♒
Color: White

Deer are associated with the Horned God.

29 Wednesday

3rd ♒
☽ v/c 10:20 am
☽ enters ♓ 8:33 pm
Color: Brown

◑ Thursday

3rd ♓
4th quarter 1:13 pm
Color: Green

Wisteria represents beauty increasing with age.

31 Friday

4th ♓
☽ v/c 10:55 pm
☽ enters ♈ 11:28 pm
Color: Purple

Purple aids intuition and authority.

Baba Darista

In the Russian village of Volodiatino lived a woman known as Baba Darista who was brought to trial in 1647. Baba Darista was a fortune-teller who came to the attention of authorities after a local man complained that his neighbor had stolen property from him, which he had learned after consulting Baba Darista.

During her interrogation, Baba Darista explained that she began her career of fortune-telling fifty years prior. She claimed that she had been ill and weak when, one day, she had a vision in church of a man who instructed her to divine for those in need. Sometime later, this man, along with a woman, appeared to her "as if coming out of water."

Baba Darista noted that her method of divination involved looking into salt. When gazing into the salt, she would see little men who would provide certain answers based on their behaviors. When pressed further, and after being subjected to torture, Baba Darista implicated others in the village as fortune-tellers. Sadly, in the end, Baba Darista was sentenced to be burned.

—Kelden

1 Saturday
4th ♈
Color: Blue

2 Sunday
4th ♈
☽ v/c 6:04 pm
Color: Gold

June

3 Monday
4th ♈
☽ enters ♉ 1:55 am
☿ enters ♊ 3:37 am
Color: Gray

*Peacocks represent confidence in your own
splendor. Don't hide what makes you awesome.*

4 Tuesday
4th ♉
Color: Maroon

5 Wednesday
4th ♉
☽ v/c 4:09 am
☽ enters ♊ 4:36 am
Color: Topaz

Wearing jade brings justice.

☽ Thursday
4th ♊
New Moon 8:38 am
Color: Crimson

*A sea drum has tiny pellets sealed inside; it can be drummed or
tilted to make wave sounds, representing both earth and water.*

7 Friday
1st ♊
☽ v/c 8:16 am
☽ enters ♋ 8:41 am
Color: White

Set in Eastern Daylight Time (EDT)

8 Saturday

1st ♋
Color: Black

Onatah is the Iroquois goddess of corn, one of the Three Sisters.

9 Sunday

1st ♋
♂ enters ♉ 12:35 am
☽ v/c 3:05 pm
☽ enters ♌ 3:29 pm
Color: Yellow

June

10 Monday
1st ♌
Color: Lavender

Celtic Tree Month of Oak begins

11 Tuesday
1st ♌
☽ v/c 3:16 pm
Color: Gray

Shavuot begins at sundown

12 Wednesday
1st ♌
☽ enters ♍ 1:39 am
Color: White

13 Thursday
1st ♍
Color: Turquoise

◑ Friday
1st ♍
2nd quarter 1:18 am
☽ v/c 1:54 pm
☽ enters ♎ 2:12 pm
Color: Rose

Flag Day

Set in Eastern Daylight Time (EDT)

Midsummer: The Power

At Midsummer, the summer solstice, our greatest heavenly body, the Sun, is at its greatest power. It's the longest day of the year. Without our Sun, the center of our universe, our planet would perish. Plants and all humanity would cease to exist.

On this sabbat celebrate the Sun's power. Begin by greeting the sunrise. See dawn break on the eastern horizon. Listen as life begins to stir. The birds don't just sing at sunrise—it's a jubilation. Soon the Sun lights the entire sky. The Sun energizes every living being.

On this sabbat begin your ritual outdoors at noon if possible. On a stable surface safely light an orange pillar candle. Gaze at the flame. On yellow or other brightly colored paper, write the name or names of a person or people who give you power. Who is at the center of your universe? A partner, spouse, children, or friend? After their name, write how they empower you. Save this list for when you need a lift. Safely extinguish the candle. At sunset think of the remarkable power our Sun has over us.

—James Kambos

15 Saturday

2nd ♎
Color: Indigo

Hawthorn is associated with the Fae.

16 Sunday

2nd ♎
Color: Orange

Father's Day

June

17 Monday
2nd ♎︎
☽ v/c 2:05 am
♀ enters ♋︎ 2:20 am
☽ enters ♏︎ 2:38 am
☿ enters ♋︎ 5:07 am
Color: Silver

18 Tuesday
2nd ♏︎
Color: Black

For protection or banishing, use black.

19 Wednesday
2nd ♏︎
☽ v/c 12:19 pm
☽ enters ♐︎ 12:32 pm
Color: Yellow

Juneteenth

20 Thursday
2nd ♐︎
☉ enters ♋︎ 4:51 pm
Color: Green

Midsummer/Litha/Summer Solstice
Sun enters Cancer

☺ Friday
2nd ♐︎
☽ v/c 6:58 pm
☽ enters ♑︎ 7:08 pm
Full Moon 9:08 pm
Color: Pink

Strong Sun Moon

Set in Eastern Daylight Time (EDT)

June Moon of Inspiration

The days are at their longest, and the Sun is king. With all the light offered, we find our surroundings wrapped in a glorious display of blooms. The scents, the colors, and the sounds of a landscape in full ripeness offer inspiration to many of us who spend time in nature. As you walk through the forest, park, beach, or even your own neighborhood, take time to stop and admire the beauty and wisdom nature has to offer.

There is a story in every petal, leaf, and stone you come upon in nature. Use the silky light of June's Full Moon to tap into your creative side. Spend some quiet time in a garden or natural setting. Take a journal and sketch or write whatever comes to you. As the Moon rises, close your eyes and focus on your entries. Where did your creative mind take you?

—Monica Crosson

---

22 Saturday
3rd ♑
Color: Gray

Palo santo is used for blessing and purification.

---

23 Sunday
3rd ♑
☽ v/c 11:05 pm
☽ enters ♒ 11:14 pm
Color: Amber

June

24 Monday
3rd ≈
Color: Ivory

A sachet of thistle speeds healing from illness or injury.

25 Tuesday
3rd ≈
☽ v/c 6:30 pm
Color: Maroon

26 Wednesday
3rd ≈
☽ enters ♓ 2:08 am
Color: White

27 Thursday
3rd ♓
Color: Crimson

Moles deal in secrets and discretion. Star-nosed moles have the most sensitive touch.

Friday
3rd ♓
☽ v/c 4:45 am
☽ enters ♈ 4:52 am
4th quarter 5:53 pm
Color: Purple

To ward a home against evil, place yucca fiber on the hearth. It can be used as tinder or twisted into cord.

Set in Eastern Daylight Time (EDT)

Fresh Garden Peas and Quinoa

Garden peas—a joy to both chef and gardener. They are delicious fresh off the vine or cooked in your favorite dish. Peas hold energy for abundance. They can be used to attract love and prosperity and to support work to aid communication and inspire creativity.

1 T. butter
1 cup quinoa, rinsed
2 cups chicken or vegetable broth
¼ cup chopped onion
1 clove garlic, minced
1 cup fresh garden peas
1 tsp. chopped fresh thyme
½ cup grated parmesan
Pepper to taste

In a saucepan, melt the butter. Stir in quinoa and cook for 2 minutes to toast. Add the broth, onion, garlic, peas, and thyme and turn up heat to bring to a boil. Then cover the pan and reduce to a simmer. Cook for 15 minutes, or until all liquid has been absorbed. Transfer to a serving dish and top with parmesan and 1 to 2 grinds of pepper. Serve hot.

—Laurel Woodward

29 Saturday

4th ♈
♄ ℞ 3:07 pm
Color: Blue

Blue brings peace, calm, and clarity.

30 Sunday

4th ♈
☽ v/c 12:56 am
☽ enters ♉ 8:00 am
Color: Gold

July 2024

S	M	T	W
	1	2	3
7	8	9	10
14	15	16	17
☺ Blessing Moon	22 Sun enters Leo	23	24
28	29	30	31
4	5	6	7

T	F	S	Notes
4	☽	6	
Independence Day			
11	12	◑	
18	19	20	
25	26	◐	
1	2	3	
8	9	10	

July

1 Monday
4th ♉
Color: Lavender

Canada Day

2 Tuesday
4th ♉
Ψ ℞ 6:40 am
☿ enters ♌ 8:50 am
☽ v/c 11:43 am
☽ enters ♊ 11:50 am
Color: Gray

3 Wednesday
4th ♊
Color: Brown

*Knockanare Well has miraculously healed
numerous people throughout Irish mythology.*

4 Thursday
4th ♊
☽ v/c 4:44 pm
☽ enters ♋ 4:51 pm
Color: Turquoise

Independence Day

Friday
4th ♋
New Moon 6:57 pm
Color: Rose

Siri Christoffersdatter

On March 14, 1655, a woman named Siri Christoffersdatter was brought to trial in Vardø, Norway. According to Christoffersdatter, she had learned Witchcraft from another woman while working on a farm. She explained that, after offering up a cow, the Devil appeared in the form of a horned man dressed in black. The Devil, who called himself Jacob, asked that Christoffersdatter serve him, which she agreed to.

The following year, Christoffersdatter began working on a different farm, where she taught Witchcraft to another woman. She explained that she passed power to this woman via a piece of flatbread. The Devil then appeared and bade the women to play cards with him, explaining that if they lost, they had to serve him. When the women did indeed lose, the Devil promised to procure for them whatever they might need.

Christoffersdatter also confessed to having shape-shifted into a raven and, along with other Witches in the forms of seals and seagulls, having sunk the ships of their enemies. Consequently, she was sentenced to death via beheading.

—Kelden

---

6 Saturday

1st ♋
☽ v/c 11:47 pm
☽ enters ♌ 11:56 pm
Color: Black

---

7 Sunday

1st ♌
Color: Yellow

Islamic New Year begins at sundown

---

8 Monday
1st ♌
Color: White

Celtic Tree Month of Holly begins

9 Tuesday
1st ♌
☽ v/c 2:04 am
☽ enters ♍ 9:48 am
Color: Red

For self-love and compassion, use freesia.

10 Wednesday
1st ♍
Color: Topaz

The serenity of loons is a reminder to pay attention to your dreams.

11 Thursday
1st ♍
♀ enters ♌ 12:19 pm
☽ v/c 9:55 pm
☽ enters ♎ 10:06 pm
Color: Purple

12 Friday
1st ♎
Color: Coral

◑ Saturday

1st ♎︎
☽ v/c 6:49 pm
2nd quarter 6:49 pm
Color: Blue

Subdue fear with sodalite.

14 Sunday

2nd ♎︎
☽ enters ♏︎ 10:53 am
Color: Amber

July

15 Monday

2nd ♏
Color: Gray

16 Tuesday

2nd ♏
☽ v/c 9:10 pm
☽ enters ♐ 9:25 pm
Color: Scarlet

For dowsing, use hazel wood.

17 Wednesday
2nd ♐
Color: Yellow

*Japanese Buddhists honor Kannon
as a bodhisattva of compassion.*

18 Thursday
2nd ♐
Color: Turquoise

19 Friday
2nd ♐
☽ v/c 3:58 am
☽ enters ♑ 4:14 am
Color: White

Nag champa incense aids meditation.

Set in Eastern Daylight Time (EDT)

July Moon of Strength

Step into the light and feel the strength of the Sun's fingers as they stretch across your face. Summer is in full glory. And just as July bears its glorious crown, festooned with the beauty of the season, remember to wear your own crown with pride. Hold your head high, empowered one, for you are divine. I know, insecurities can creep up and cause us to doubt our own courage, but please be kind to the one who looks back at you in the mirror. Give yourself  praise for the wins of the day and shake off the losses. Remember you are a badass warrior who can take on anything.

On the evening of July's Full Moon, stand beneath its crowning rays with your arms outstretched. Proclaim yourself a divine warrior. Celebrate your strength and vitality with dance, drumming, or chanting.

—Monica Crosson

20 Saturday
2nd ♑
♂ enters ♊ 4:43 pm
Color: Indigo

☺ Sunday
2nd ♑
Full Moon 6:17 am
☽ v/c 7:26 am
☽ enters ♒ 7:43 am
Color: Orange

Blessing Moon

July

22 Monday

3rd ≈
☉ enters ♌ 3:44 am
Color: Silver

Sun enters Leo

23 Tuesday

3rd ≈
☽ v/c 5:58 am
☽ enters ♓ 9:23 am
Color: Maroon

Meet challenges with carnelian.

24 Wednesday

3rd ♓
Color: White

25 Thursday

3rd ♓
☽ v/c 10:31 am
☽ enters ♈ 10:52 am
☿ enters ♍ 6:42 pm
Color: Crimson

26 Friday

3rd ♈
♀ ℞ 9:59 am
☽ v/c 6:14 pm
Color: Pink

To fight nightmares, use wood betony.

Set in Eastern Daylight Time (EDT)

Plum Crumb Cake

½ cup butter, softened, plue more for pan
½ cup sugar
2 eggs
¼ cup sour cream
1 tsp. vanilla extract
1½ cups flour
1 tsp. baking powder
¼ tsp. salt
½ tsp. cinnamon
¼ tsp. nutmeg
3 cups fresh plums sliced into eighths
Juice of 1 lemon
¼ cup sugar
2 T. cold butter, cut into small chunks

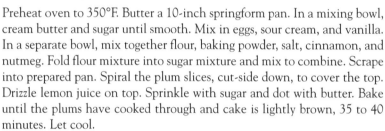

Preheat oven to 350°F. Butter a 10-inch springform pan. In a mixing bowl, cream butter and sugar until smooth. Mix in eggs, sour cream, and vanilla. In a separate bowl, mix together flour, baking powder, salt, cinnamon, and nutmeg. Fold flour mixture into sugar mixture and mix to combine. Scrape into prepared pan. Spiral the plum slices, cut-side down, to cover the top. Drizzle lemon juice on top. Sprinkle with sugar and dot with butter. Bake until the plums have cooked through and cake is lightly brown, 35 to 40 minutes. Let cool.

—Laurel Woodward

◑ Saturday
3rd ♈
☽ enters ♉ 1:23 pm
4th quarter 10:52 pm
Color: Gray

*For help setting boundaries, turn to
geese, who make fantastic guardians.*

---

28 Sunday
4th ♉
Color: Gold

August 2024

S	M	T	W
☽	5	6	7
	Mercury Retrograde		
11	◐	13	14
18	☺	20	21
	Corn Moon		
25	◑	27	28
			Mercury Direct
1	2	3	4

T	F	S	
1	2	3	**Notes**
Lammas/Lughnasadh			_____
8	9	10	_____
			_____
15	16	17	_____
			_____
22	23	24	_____
Sun enters Virgo			_____
29	30	31	_____
			_____
5	6	7	_____
			_____

July/August

29 Monday

4th ♉
☽ v/c 4:59 pm
☽ enters ♊ 5:28 pm
Color: Ivory

30 Tuesday

4th ♊
Color: Gray

Sweet pea makes the wearer irresistible.

31 Wednesday

4th ♊
☽ v/c 10:46 pm
☽ enters ♋ 11:19 pm
Color: Topaz

1 Thursday

4th ♋
Color: Green

Lammas/Lughnasadh

2 Friday

4th ♋
Color: Rose

Set in Eastern Daylight Time (EDT)

Lughnasadh: The Ripening

Lughnasadh is the sabbat that marks the first harvest. A sweet serenity settles across the farmlands. The ripening has begun. Grapes not yet ready for harvest hang in clusters. The first corn comes to market and grains begin to reach harvest stage.

County fairs are held about now, farmer's markets begin to feature fresh produce, and backyard gardens begin to yield their bounty. This is also the time when ancient Pagans honored agricultural deities such as Diana.

Modern Witches can still reach back on this sabbat and connect with our ancient rural roots. Instead of an organized ritual, try getting in touch with the land in some manner. Attend a county fair. Visit a farmer's market or an orchard. Don't forget to stop at a roadside stand and buy a loaf of homemade bread. When you get home, serve the produce and baked goods. Let your kitchen counter become your altar. Mindfully eat and enjoy these gifts from the earth.

The haste of early summer growth has ended. Nature pauses. The golden days of the ripening are upon us.

—James Kambos

---

3 Saturday

4th ♋
☽ v/c 6:31 am
☽ enters ♌ 7:10 am
Color: Black

The Zamzam well in Mecca is sacred to Islam.

☽ Sunday

4th ♌
New Moon 7:13 am
♀ enters ♍ 10:23 pm
Color: Yellow

Rhubarb promotes fidelity.

---

5 Monday

1st ♌
☿ ℞ 12:56 am
☽ v/c 11:16 am
☽ enters ♍ 5:17 pm
Color: Gray

Celtic Tree Month of Hazel begins
Mercury retrograde until August 28

6 Tuesday

1st ♍
Color: Black

Lammas cross-quarter day (Sun reaches 15° Leo)

7 Wednesday

1st ♍
Color: White

8 Thursday

1st ♍
☽ v/c 4:40 am
☽ enters ♎ 5:31 am
Color: Purple

For knowledge, use apatite.

9 Friday

1st ♎
☽ v/c 5:45 pm
Color: Pink

Gwen ferch Ellis

Gwen ferch Ellis, a Welsh folk healer, came under suspicion of Witchcraft in the early summer of 1594. Ellis was well known in her community for her ability to heal humans and animals alike. However, she ran into trouble when a written charm was discovered in the home of the well-to-do Mostyn family. The charm, which was said to be Ellis's creation, was written backward—which was believed to signify a malefic intention.

When questioned, Ellis admitted that she had learned charming from her late sister. However, she fervently denied having created or placed the charm in the Mostyn home. She did admit to having seen a similar charm in the prayer book of Jane Conway, whose family had been fighting with the Mostyns. Conway was well acquainted with Ellis and had supposedly approached her for help getting revenge on Thomas Mostyn.

That July, seven witnesses came forward to denounce Ellis as a Witch. Three months later in October, Ellis was sentenced to hang, becoming the first person to be executed for Witchcraft in Wales.

—Kelden

---

10 Saturday
1st ♎
☽ enters ♏ 6:34 pm
Color: Brown

---

11 Sunday
1st ♏
Color: Amber

Acacia represents divine authority and immortality.

Monday

1st ♏

2nd quarter 11:19 am

Color: Silver

13 Tuesday

2nd ♏

☽ v/c 5:01 am

☽ enters ♐ 6:01 am

Color: White

Ogmios is the Gaulish god of communication and ogham.

14 Wednesday

2nd ♐

☿ enters ♌ 8:16 pm

Color: Yellow

15 Thursday

2nd ♐

☽ v/c 12:52 pm

☽ enters ♑ 1:51 pm

Color: Crimson

Woodwinds embody the element of air.

16 Friday

2nd ♑

Color: Coral

Egyptian musk incense promotes peace and calm.

17 Saturday
2nd ♑
☽ v/c 4:43 pm
☽ enters ♒ 5:45 pm
Color: Gray

18 Sunday
2nd ♒
Color: Orange

Use orange to boost creative genius.

August

☺ **Monday**

2nd ♒

☽ v/c 2:26 pm

Full Moon 2:26 pm

☽ enters ♓ 6:52 pm

Color: Lavender

Corn Moon

---

20 Tuesday

3rd ♓

Color: Maroon

For reconnecting with the departed, use black-eyed Susans.

---

21 Wednesday

3rd ♓

☽ v/c 5:54 pm

☽ enters ♈ 7:02 pm

Color: Topaz

---

22 Thursday

3rd ♈

☉ enters ♍ 10:55 am

Color: White

Sun enters Virgo

---

23 Friday

3rd ♈

☽ v/c 8:44 am

☽ enters ♉ 8:00 pm

Color: Purple

*Clootie wells are found throughout Celtic territory,
distinguished by trees full of rags tied for healing prayers.*

Set in Eastern Daylight Time (EDT)

August Moon of Gathering

Let us gather in circles to celebrate the gifts Mother Earth has provided. This once-laborious time of harvest and preparation for the long winter months was shared by family and neighboring farmers to make the work less tedious and was always followed by large gatherings to celebrate a work well done. Creating community is an important aspect of our lives, as it promotes a sense of belonging and rejuvenates the spirit. It's easy to allow friendship to take a backseat in our busy lives, but carving out just a little bit of time to develop and maintain healthy friendships is good for your body, mind, and soul.

Under the golden glow of August's Full Moon, gather with like-minded friends to acknowledge the gifts that Mother Earth has provided. Share local ale and homemade bread, scones, or berry cobbler. Eat, drink, and be merry.

—Monica Crosson

24 Saturday

3rd ♉
Color: Indigo

25 Sunday

3rd ♉
☽ v/c 9:40 pm
☽ enters ♊ 11:04 pm
Color: Yellow

Frogs are sacred to Hecate.

◑ Monday

3rd ♊
4th quarter 5:26 am
Color: White

27 Tuesday

4th ♊
Color: Gray

Chichen Itza is considered a gateway to the watery underworld.

28 Wednesday

4th ♊
☽ v/c 3:14 am
☽ enters ♋ 4:47 am
☿ D 5:14 pm
Color: Brown

Mercury direct

29 Thursday

4th ♋
♀ enters ♎ 9:23 am
Color: Purple

30 Friday

4th ♋
☽ v/c 11:24 am
☽ enters ♌ 1:09 pm
Color: White

Nightingales lift low spirits and lighten the darkness.

Tomato Mozzarella Pizza

2½ cups flour
1 tsp. salt
½ tsp. sugar
½ tsp. yeast
3 T. olive oil
¾ cup water
Sauce
Fresh or shredded mozzarella
Tomato slices, fresh or roasted

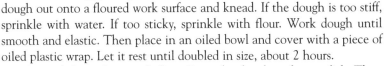

In a mixing bowl, mix together dry ingredients. Make a well and add oil and water. Mix until a shaggy dough forms. Turn dough out onto a floured work surface and knead. If the dough is too stiff, sprinkle with water. If too sticky, sprinkle with flour. Work dough until smooth and elastic. Then place in an oiled bowl and cover with a piece of oiled plastic wrap. Let it rest until doubled in size, about 2 hours.

Dust a baking sheet with flour. Press the dough to form a disk. Then stretch it as you turn it. Set it on a baking sheet and cover with parchment paper. Use a rolling pin to roll the dough as thin as possible.

Heat oven to 500°F. Top the dough with your favorite sauce, mozzarella, and fresh or oven-roasted tomatoes. Bake 10 to 15 minutes (a thicker crust requires a longer bake time). Serve hot.

—Laurel Woodward

---

31 Saturday

4th ♌
Color: Blue

Go-away-evil incense is for banishing and hex-breaking.

1 Sunday

4th ♌
♅ ℞ 11:18 am
♀ enters ♑ 8:10 pm
☽ v/c 8:25 pm
☽ enters ♍ 11:48 pm
Color: Gold

September 2024

S	M	T	W
1	2 ☽	3	4
	Labor Day		
8	9	10	11 ◐
15	16	17 ☺	18
		Harvest Moon Lunar Eclipse	
22	23	24 ◑	25
Mabon / Fall Equinox Sun enters Libra			
29	30	1	2
6	7	8	9

T	F	S	
5	6	7	**Notes**
12	13	14	
19	20	21	
26	27	28	
3	4	5	
10	11	10	

September

☽ Monday
4th ♍
New Moon 9:56 pm
Color: Lavender

Labor Day
Labour Day (Canada)
Celtic Tree Month of Vine begins

3 Tuesday
1st ♍
Color: Black

Bats symbolize rebirth and assist in past-life work.

4 Wednesday
1st ♍
☽ v/c 12:06 pm
☽ enters ♎ 12:12 pm
♂ enters ♋ 3:46 pm
Color: White

5 Thursday
1st ♎
Color: Green

Bleeding heart deals in emotional pain and healing.

6 Friday
1st ♎
Color: Pink

Alice Duke

In the winter of 1664, Alice Duke of Somerset, England, was arrested and examined on suspicion of being a Witch. Duke confessed that just over a decade prior, she had been convinced by Ann Bishop to go to the churchyard at night. There, the two women walked backward around the church three times. After their first circling, the Devil appeared to them as a man dressed in black. The second time, a great black toad material-

ized, and the third time a rat. After this, Bishop told Duke that she would have whatever she desired.

Later, the Devil appeared to Duke and repeated that she would want for nothing. The Devil explained that she only needed to sell her soul to him, give offerings of her blood, and do mischief. Duke agreed to these terms, at which point the Devil pricked the fourth finger on her right hand. He gave her a pen and directed her to sign a piece of parchment with her blood. Upon her doing so, the Devil gave Duke a sixpence and vanished.

—Kelden

7 Saturday

1st ♎
☽ v/c 1:08 am
☽ enters ♏ 1:18 am
Color: Gray

Wrens are associated with creativity, music, and the arts.

8 Sunday

1st ♏
Color: Yellow

September

9 Monday

1st ♏
☿ enters ♍ 2:50 am
☽ v/c 1:11 pm
☽ enters ♐ 1:26 pm
Color: Ivory

10 Tuesday

1st ♐
Color: White

A didgeridoo is a long hollow tube that makes resonant sounds, said to tie the world together.

◑ Wednesday

1st ♐
2nd quarter 2:06 am
☽ v/c 8:21 pm
☽ enters ♑ 10:38 pm
Color: Brown

Binding spells work well with onyx or obsidian.

12 Thursday

2nd ♑
Color: Turquoise

13 Friday

2nd ♑
Color: Rose

Set in Eastern Daylight Time (EDT)

Mabon: The Bounty

The sabbat of Mabon observes the autumn equinox. It's a time of Thanksgiving for the bounty of the earth and a time to observe nature's decline into the dark season.

Mabon means "Great Son." As the legend goes, Mabon, the son of the Goddess, was abducted as a child and taken to the land of Avalon. He was freed and returned as a young man. The legend is used to explain nature's decline in autumn and its return at Ostara. Even though we are entering the dark season, we're surrounded with bounty. Country markets overflow with pumpkins, apples, and autumn flowers.

To celebrate this time of bounty, decorate your altar with seasonal décor—pumpkins, mums, and leaves are ideas. Then in your Book of Shadows write down the bounty you're grateful for—family, home, career, etc. Leave your book open for a few days. Then review your list. Send loving thoughts out to the people and things on your list. Put your book away.

The chill comes and the fingers of dusk draw earlier across the land, but we are surrounded by the bounty of Mabon.

—James Kambos

---

14 Saturday

2nd ♑
☽ v/c 3:35 am
☽ enters ♒ 3:53 am
Color: Blue

Vodou invokes La Sirene, the mermaid loa of the sea.

---

15 Sunday

2nd ♒
Color: Orange

Old yews grow in churchyards and other sacred sites. The Fortingall Yew in Perthshire is believed to be over 5,000 years old.

September

16 Monday

2nd ≈
☽ v/c 1:04 am
☽ enters ♓ 5:39 am
Color: Silver

☺ Tuesday

2nd ♓
Full Moon 10:34 pm
Color: Gray

Harvest Moon
Lunar Eclipse, 10:34 pm, 25° ♓ 41'

18 Wednesday

3rd ♓
☽ v/c 5:02 am
☽ enters ♈ 5:24 am
Color: Topaz

19 Thursday

3rd ♈
Color: Crimson

Seven chakras is a set of seven incense
blends to activate each of the chakras.

20 Friday

3rd ♈
☽ v/c 4:39 am
☽ enters ♉ 5:03 am
Color: Coral

Set in Eastern Daylight Time (EDT)

September Moon of Wisdom

The light shifts as the wheel turns. Shadows grow long across dewy fields, and day and night are once again equal in length. We glean the fields and prepare ourselves for the dark days ahead. Before we look ahead to that busy time of autumn and winter celebrations, we should take time to pause and look back and honor the lessons we have learned throughout the passing year.

As you prepare for the descent into the dark half of the year, pull out a journal and sit quietly under September's Full Moon. Contemplate the wisdom you've gleaned from nature, from others, or from yourself. What intentions did you plant at the beginning of this year? What goals came to fruition? What have you learned about yourself? Remember to add your victories big and small, quotes that impacted you in some way, or even the lines from a memorable song.

—Monica Crosson

21 Saturday

3rd ☉
Color: Black

UN International Day of Peace

22 Sunday

3rd ☉
☽ v/c 6:14 am
☽ enters ♊ 6:24 am
☉ enters ♎ 8:44 am
♀ enters ♏ 10:36 pm
Color: Gold

Mabon/Fall Equinox
Sun enters Libra

September

23 Monday
3rd ♊
Color: Gray

Sweetgrass cleanses and summons spirits.

◑ Tuesday
3rd ♊
☽ v/c 7:59 am
☽ enters ♋ 10:50 am
4th quarter 2:50 pm
Color: Scarlet

25 Wednesday
4th ♋
Color: Yellow

Malachite is a good money stone.

26 Thursday
4th ♋
☿ enters ♎ 4:09 am
☽ v/c 6:12 pm
☽ enters ♌ 6:47 pm
Color: White

Lilies attract benevolent spirits.

27 Friday
4th ♌
Color: Purple

28 Saturday

4th ♌
☽ v/c 11:36 pm
Color: Indigo

29 Sunday

4th ♌
☽ enters ♍ 5:42 am
Color: Amber

October 2024

S	M	T	W
		1	☽
			Solar Eclipse
6	7	8	9
13	14	15	16
20	21	22	23
		Sun enters Scorpio	
27	28	29	30
3	4	5	6

T	F	S	
3	4	5	**Notes**
◐	11	12	
☺ (Blood Moon)	18	19	
◑	25	26	
31 Samhain Halloween	1	2	
7	8	9	

September/October

30 Monday
4th ♍
Color: White

Celtic Tree Month of Ivy begins

1 Tuesday
4th ♍
☽ v/c 5:39 pm
☽ enters ♎ 6:20 pm
Color: Red

Red relates to sex and seduction.

☽ Wednesday
4th ♎
New Moon 2:49 pm
Color: Brown

Rosh Hashanah begins at sundown
Solar Eclipse, 2:49 pm, 10° ♎ 04'

3 Thursday
1st ♎
Color: Turquoise

4 Friday
1st ♎
☽ v/c 6:40 am
☽ enters ♏ 7:22 am
Color: Coral

126   *Set in Eastern Daylight Time (EDT)*

Blackberry Oat Bars

1 cup old-fashioned rolled oats
½ cup chopped walnuts
1 cup flour
⅔ cup brown sugar, packed
½ tsp. salt
½ cup butter, plus more for pan
4 cups fresh blackberries
2 T. water
½ cup sugar
¼ cup lemon juice
½ tsp. cinnamon
4 tsp. cornstarch

Butter a 9 × 9-inch pan. Grind oats and walnuts to create a meal. In a mixing bowl, stir flour, brown sugar, and salt into oat mixture. Cut in butter and mix to form coarse crumbs. Spoon half the crumbs into the prepared pan and press to form a crust. Place the pan and the remaining crumbs in refrigerator to firm. For filling, place blackberries and water in a medium saucepan and sprinkle sugar, lemon juice, cinnamon, and cornstarch over them. Bring to a boil, then reduce to a simmer. Cook about 8 minutes, stirring frequently, until thickened. Remove from heat and cool to room temperature. Heat oven to 350°F. Spread berry filling over crust and top with remaining crumbs. Bake 35 to 40 minutes, or until the fruit boils up around the edges. Transfer to a rack to cool.

—Laurel Woodward

5 Saturday

1st ♏
Color: Gray

Herons symbolize patience and independence.

6 Sunday

1st ♏
☽ v/c 6:52 pm
☽ enters ♐ 7:34 pm
Color: Orange

October

7 Monday
1st ✗
Color: Ivory

8 Tuesday
1st ✗
Color: White

*The Nuragic holy well is a Sardinian structure
from the Bronze Age devoted to worshipping waters.*

9 Wednesday
1st ✗
☽ v/c 1:54 am
♃ ℞ 3:05 am
☽ enters ♑ 5:38 am
Color: Topaz

*Divino Niño Jesus incense blesses
children and honors child gods.*

◑ Thursday
1st ♑
2nd quarter 2:55 pm
Color: Purple

11 Friday
2nd ♑
☽ v/c 11:53 am
☽ enters ♒ 12:31 pm
♀ D 8:34 pm
Color: White

Yom Kippur begins at sundown

12 Saturday
2nd ≈
Color: Brown

The secrets of the night belong to owls.

13 Sunday
2nd ≈
☽ v/c 10:11 am
☿ enters ♏ 3:23 pm
☽ enters ♓ 3:55 pm
Color: Gold

October

14 Monday
2nd ♓
Color: Silver

Indigenous Peoples' Day
Thanksgiving Day (Canada)

15 Tuesday
2nd ♓
☽ v/c 4:00 pm
☽ enters ♈ 4:34 pm
Color: Gray

16 Wednesday
2nd ♈
Color: White

Sukkot begins at sundown

☺ Thursday
2nd ♈
Full Moon 7:26 am
☽ v/c 3:26 pm
♀ enters ♐ 3:28 pm
☽ enters ♉ 4:00 pm
Color: Green

Blood Moon

18 Friday
3rd ♉
Color: Rose

October Moon of Thresholds

October brings with it a glorious trans-formation that is both exhilarating and melancholy, as we realize we have truly come into the dark half of the year. Once again, the veil thins, and we may feel the tendrils of the otherworld as they slip through the curtain. This is a time of mystery and magick, a time of reflection and shedding of those things that no longer serve us. As we cross the threshold of October, we acknowledge change and accept the Crone's dark mantle with gratitude.

Under the glow of October's Full Moon, find acceptance of change by meditating with your favorite incense blend. Honor the wisdom of dark Crone energy as you reflect on those things that have served you well and acknowledge the lessons learned from those things that did not.

—Monica Crosson

19 Saturday

3rd ♉
☽ v/c 3:33 pm
☽ enters ♊ 4:07 pm
Color: Blue

20 Sunday

3rd ♊
Color: Yellow

Yellow brings abundance and joy, like a burst of sunshine.

October

21 Monday

3rd ♊
☽ v/c 5:00 pm
☽ enters ♋ 6:50 pm
Color: White

22 Tuesday

3rd ♋
☉ enters ♏ 6:15 pm
Color: Maroon

Sun enters Scorpio

23 Wednesday

3rd ♋
Color: Brown

Sukkot ends

◑ Thursday

3rd ♋
☽ v/c 12:47 am
☽ enters ♌ 1:24 am
4th quarter 4:03 am
Color: Crimson

Healing comes from hematite.

25 Friday

4th ♌
Color: Pink

Set in Eastern Daylight Time (EDT)

Johannes Junius

On July 5, 1628, Johannes Junius of Bamberg, Germany, confessed to Witchcraft. Junius claimed that four years prior, he had encountered a mysterious woman while in his orchard. The woman seduced Junius before suddenly turning into a goat, who was revealed to be the Devil. The goat demanded that Junius renounce Christ, which he did not. However, when the Devil appeared again, Junius agreed to renounce his faith. He was rebaptized, given the name Krix, and granted a spirit called Vixen. Junius recounted how Vixen had urged him to murder his two children, but he refused and was beaten.

Junius was able to smuggle a letter to his daughter in which he recanted his confession, explaining that it was a result of the unbearable torture he had endured. In the letter he writes, "Innocent have I come into prison, innocent have I been tortured, innocent must I die. For whoever comes into the witch prison must become a witch or be tortured until he invents something out of his head."

—Kelden

26 Saturday
4th ♌
☽ v/c 4:04 am
☽ enters ♍ 11:47 am
Color: Indigo

Squirrels excel at gauging risks and benefits as
they hurtle through the heights of the forest.

27 Sunday
4th ♍
Color: Amber

November 2024

S	M	T	W
3 Daylight Saving Time ends at 2 am	4	5 Election Day (general)	6
10	11	12	13
17	18	19	20
24	25 Mercury Retrograde	26	27
1	2	3	4

T	F	S	
	☽	2	**Notes**
7	8	◐	
14	☺	16	
	Mourning Moon		
21	◑	23	
Sun enters Sagittarius			
28	29	30	
Thanksgiving Day			
5	6	7	

28 Monday
4th ♍
☽ v/c 11:54 pm
Color: Gray

Celtic Tree Month of Reed begins

29 Tuesday
4th ♍
☽ enters ♎ 12:30 am
Color: Scarlet

30 Wednesday
4th ♎
Color: White

31 Thursday
4th ♎
☽ v/c 12:57 pm
☽ enters ♏ 1:29 pm
Color: Purple

Samhain/Halloween

☽ Friday
4th ♏
New Moon 8:47 am
Color: Coral

All Saints' Day

Samhain: The Shadows

Samhain is the final harvest. The fields are mostly bare. The shadows fall early across meadows and suburban lawns. But they aren't the only shadows to be found on Samhain. We are also in the shadow of the spirit realm. As dusk forgets the light of day, the shadows of the night are active with spirits. Some of these shadows carry with them the spirits of our beloved ancestors.

On this Night of Shadows, you may connect with your ancestors. Cover your altar with black fabric. Place photos of your deceased loved ones on your altar. Near the center place one red apple. Ground and center. Whisper the name of one loved one. Close your eyes. Do you see or hear anything? Continue for as long as you wish. When done, place the apple outside your door. The next day compost it or throw it away.

The shadows deepen. The bare trees creak in the wind. The candle in the jack-o'-lantern burns low. On Samhain the spirits of our ancestors are always near, in the Shadows of the Night.

—James Kambos

2 Saturday

1st ♏
☿ enters ♐ 3:18 pm
Color: Black

3 Sunday

1st ♏
☽ v/c 12:51 am
☽ enters ♐ 1:19 am
♂ enters ♌ 11:10 pm
Color: Yellow

Daylight Saving Time ends at 2 am

November

4 Monday

1st ♐
Color: Ivory

Drums represent the heartbeat of Mother Earth.

5 Tuesday

1st ♐
☽ v/c 5:23 am
☽ enters ♑ 10:17 am
Color: White

Election Day (general)

6 Wednesday

1st ♑
Color: Topaz

7 Thursday

1st ♑
☽ v/c 5:38 pm
☽ enters ♒ 5:58 pm
Color: Green

Samhain cross-quarter day (Sun reaches 15° Scorpio)

8 Friday

1st ♒
Color: Rose

Set in Eastern Standard Time (EST)

Butternut Squash Fries

1 butternut squash
3 T. olive oil
1 T. rosemary
½ tsp. salt
¼ tsp. garlic powder (optional)
1–2 grinds of pepper

Preheat oven to 425°F. Lightly spray a baking sheet with a nonstick cooking spray and set aside. Take your squash and slice off the top and the bottom. With a sharp knife or a peeler, remove the skin. Slice the squash in half and remove the seeds. Then cut the squash, slicing it into fry-size planks. Put the squash slices into a large bowl and drizzle lightly with olive oil. Sprinkle the rosemary, salt, garlic powder, and pepper over the squash and turn to coat so that each piece is covered. Spread the squash pieces over the baking sheet in a single layer. Bake for 25 minutes, or until lightly browned. You can also use an air fryer and cook in batches. Run the air fryer for 5 minutes at 390°F. Place a portion of the squash fries into the basket and cook 12 to 15 minutes, pausing to shake the basket several times during the process. Serve hot.

—Laurel Woodward

☽ Saturday

1st ≈
2nd quarter 12:55 am
☽ v/c 7:23 pm
☽ enters ♓ 11:00 pm
Color: Gray

Gray is balancing and moderating.

10 Sunday

2nd ♓
Color: Gold

November

11 Monday
2nd ♓
♀ enters ♑ 1:26 pm
Color: Lavender

Veterans Day
Remembrance Day (Canada)

12 Tuesday
2nd ♓
☽ v/c 1:13 am
☽ enters ♈ 1:26 am
Color: Black

13 Wednesday
2nd ♈
Color: Yellow

*Axomama is the Incan goddess of
potatoes, an ideal patroness for gardeners.*

14 Thursday
2nd ♈
☽ v/c 1:50 am
☽ enters ♉ 1:59 am
Color: White

Friday
2nd ♉
♄ D 9:20 am
Full Moon 4:28 pm
Color: Purple

Mourning Moon

Set in Eastern Standard Time (EST)

November Moon of Loss

Autumn is the season of letting go. Memories of summer still linger as the last of the leaves fall, leaving only bare trees that seem to scratch desperately at a vacant sky. Gone is the birdsong and the drone of bees. Gone is the wild energy that kept our spirits high, leaving us with an emptiness that all the warmth of a fire and tea cannot seem to fill. This, of course, is analogous to life, as letting go of the past can be hard. But, in fact, it is one of the most courageous acts we can do for ourselves.

Under the gentle light of November's Full Moon, write down those dark things from your past that you cannot change on scraps of paper and burn them in a small fire. This is your reminder that though we cannot change the past, we can dictate a better future.

—Monica Crosson

---

16 Saturday

3rd ♉
☽ v/c 2:03 am
☽ enters ♊ 2:09 am
Color: Blue

*China rain is a soothing incense
with watery associations.*

---

17 Sunday

3rd ♊
☽ v/c 11:09 pm
Color: Orange

November

18 Monday

3rd ♊
☽ enters ♋ 3:50 am
Color: Silver

19 Tuesday

3rd ♋
♀ enters ♒ 3:29 pm
Color: Gray

Horns call out to the element of fire.

20 Wednesday

3rd ♋
☽ v/c 6:20 am
☽ enters ♌ 8:51 am
Color: White

21 Thursday

3rd ♌
☉ enters ♐ 2:56 pm
Color: Turquoise

Sun enters Sagittarius

☽ Friday

3rd ♌
☽ v/c 8:15 am
☽ enters ♍ 6:01 pm
4th quarter 8:28 pm
Color: Pink

*Harebell is associated with magic
and with rabbits or hares.*

Set in Eastern Standard Time (EST)

23 Saturday
4th ♍
Color: Indigo

Indigo is for enlightenment and wisdom.

24 Sunday
4th ♍
Color: Gold

November

25 Monday
4th ♍
☽ v/c 12:35 am
☽ enters ♎ 6:20 am
☿ ℞ 9:42 pm
Color: Ivory

Celtic Tree Month of Elder begins
Mercury retrograde until December 15

26 Tuesday
4th ♎
Color: Scarlet

27 Wednesday
4th ♎
☽ v/c 4:14 am
☽ enters ♏ 7:21 pm
Color: Brown

Many Yoruban people worship Yemaya as
the river goddess who oversees childbirth.

28 Thursday
4th ♏
Color: Crimson

Thanksgiving Day (US)

29 Friday
4th ♏
Color: Rose

Persimmon Jam

Persimmons are a lovely fall fruit with joyful, festive energy for healing, love, prosperity, and self-realization.

6 large Fuyu persimmons, very ripe
1 cup sugar
2 T. lemon juice
1 T. cornstarch
2 T. orange juice

Wash, peel, and seed the persimmons. Discard the skin and seeds. Cut the fruit into small pieces. Then place the persimmon pieces into a food processor and puree. Pour the puree into a saucepan and heat over medium-high heat. Stir in the sugar and lemon juice and heat to a gentle boil. Reduce heat to a simmer, stirring occasionally.

In a separate bowl, stir the cornstarch into the orange juice until it is dissolved. Then stir the mixture into the hot jam. Continue to cook for about 15 minutes. Once the texture has thickened, remove from heat and let cool for 5 minutes. Spoon into hot sterilized jars and seal. Makes about 3 cups.

—Laurel Woodward

30 Saturday

4th ♏
☽ v/c 1:19 am
☽ enters ♐ 6:53 am
Color: Blue

☽ Sunday

4th ♐
New Moon 1:21 am
Color: Amber

For adaptability, connect with the eel.

December 2024

S	M	T	W
☽	2	3	4
◑	9	10	11
☺ Long Nights Moon Mercury Direct	16	17	18
◐	23	24 Christmas Eve	25 Christmas Day
29	☽	31 New Year's Eve	1
5	6	7	8

T	F	S	**Notes**
5	6	7	
12	13	14	
19	20	21 Yule / Winter Solstice Sun enters Capricorn	
26	27	28	
2	3	4	
9	10	11	

December

2 Monday

1st ♐
☽ v/c 10:47 am
☽ enters ♑ 4:09 pm
Color: Gray

3 Tuesday

1st ♑
Color: Maroon

African daisies boost magical power and psychic abilities.

4 Wednesday

1st ♑
☽ v/c 6:34 pm
☽ enters ♒ 11:21 pm
Color: Yellow

5 Thursday

1st ♒
Color: White

The Sacred Cenote is a Mayan
sinkhole formerly used for sacrifice.

6 Friday

1st ♒
♂ ℞ 6:33 pm
☽ v/c 7:01 pm
Color: Coral

Mars retrograde until February 23

Issobell Smyth

Tried and executed in 1661, Issobell Smyth of Forfar, Scotland, confessed that she had sold her soul to the Devil in exchange for the power to wrong those who had wronged her, or anyone else she so desired. She noted that the Devil had also promised her three halfpennies a year, which she expressed was little gain in return for her soul.

Smyth confessed that she and her coven met with the Devil every quarter of the year at "Candlemas, Rudday, Lambemas, and Hallowmas." These Christian holy days are echoed in the confessions of several other accused Scottish Witches, but it's only in Smyth's that all four are mentioned together. Interestingly, these dates would become the basis of the modern Wiccan/Neopagan Wheel of the Year: Candlemas (Imbolc), Rudday (Beltane), Lambemas (Lughnasadh), Hallowmas (Samhain).

Smyth also confessed to having magically caused harm to others. For example, she admitted to killing a man, who had previously struck her, by placing her hand on his back and wishing that he would never be able to harm another.

—Kelden

---

7 Saturday

1st ♒
♀ enters ♒ 1:13 am
☽ enters ♓ 4:49 am
♆ D 6:43 pm
Color: Brown

Sparrows are humble and communal.

◐ Sunday

1st ♓
2nd quarter 10:27 am
Color: Yellow

December

9 Monday
2nd ♓
☽ v/c 3:45 am
☽ enters ♈ 8:38 am
Color: White

Morning glory represents awakening and new beginnings.

10 Tuesday
2nd ♈
☽ v/c 5:13 pm
Color: Red

11 Wednesday
2nd ♈
☽ enters ♉ 10:55 am
Color: Brown

Magpies are magical and intelligent,
excellent for solving problems.

12 Thursday
2nd ♉
Color: Purple

Hattic mythology upholds Telepinu as the god of farming.

13 Friday
2nd ♉
☽ v/c 7:39 am
☽ enters ♊ 12:22 pm
Color: Rose

December Moon of Hope

It is the rhythms of nature that sometimes assure us that we can carry on when we feel our most vulnerable. Just the knowledge that the Sun will surely rise when we're experiencing our darkest nights, or that spring will allow us a chance at a new beginning, gives us hope. So during the darkest days of the year, be mindful of the seeds that are safely tucked under the surface. They need this time of dormancy—as do you.

The Full Moon in December sits high on our landscape and illuminates the stillness of not only the land, but also our spirit. Gift yourself the freedom to hope, to heal, to go within. Use this time of darkness to scry using a black mirror that has been cleansed with herbal infused water (try mugwort). Keep a notebook and write down your visions.

—Monica Crosson

14 Saturday

2nd ♊
Color: Gray

☺ Sunday

2nd ♊
Full Moon 4:02 am
☽ v/c 9:32 am
☽ enters ♋ 2:21 pm
☿ D 3:56 pm
Color: Gold

Long Nights Moon
Mercury direct

December

16 Monday
3rd ♋
Color: Silver

17 Tuesday
3rd ♋
☽ v/c 1:33 pm
☽ enters ♌ 6:39 pm
Color: Gray

For transmutation, use tupelo wood.

18 Wednesday
3rd ♌
Color: White

19 Thursday
3rd ♌
Color: Turquoise

*Ga-Gaah is the Iroquois god of
wisdom, the Wise Old Crow.*

20 Friday
3rd ♌
☽ v/c 12:19 am
☽ enters ♍ 2:37 am
Color: Pink

Set in Eastern Standard Time (EST)

Yule: The Hope

At Yule, on the winter solstice, we arrive at the longest night of the year. This joyous sabbat marks the birth of the Sun God. Yule is the origin of the Christian celebration of Christmas. Pagans and Christians find a common bond now as we observe a season filled with hope and peace. Homes are decorated with symbols of light and everlasting life. Lights, glittering ornaments, evergreen trees, and wreaths are symbols of this theme. Ancient peoples saw Yule as a time of hope. After a period of dark days and leafless trees, people were filled with a sense of hope. The daylight hours began to lengthen and the evergreens reminded them that life would continue.

Hopes, dreams for the future, are key elements in the Yule observance. On this darkest night of the year decorate your altar with a seasonal theme. Pine branches interwoven with white lights, and silver ornaments echo the theme of life everlasting and divinity. Sit with family and friends. Allow each person to announce the hope or dream they have. End by exchanging small gifts. Serve cocoa, eggnog, and ginger cookies!

—James Kambos

---

21 Saturday
3rd ♍
☉ enters ♑ 4:21 am
Color: Blue

Yule/Winter Solstice
Sun enters Capricorn

◐ Sunday
3rd ♍
☽ v/c 8:27 am
☽ enters ♎ 2:08 pm
4th quarter 5:18 pm
Color: Orange

Finches are fast-paced and optimistic.

December

23 Monday
4th ♎
Color: Lavender

Between (Celtic Tree Month)

24 Tuesday
4th ♎
☽ v/c 5:44 am
Color: White

Christmas Eve
Celtic Tree Month of Birch begins

25 Wednesday
4th ♎
☽ enters ♏ 3:06 am
Color: Topaz

Christmas Day
Hanukkah begins at sundown

26 Thursday
4th ♏
Color: Green

Kwanzaa begins
Boxing Day (Canada and UK)

27 Friday
4th ♏
☽ v/c 9:24 am
☽ enters ♐ 2:46 pm
Color: White

Set in Eastern Standard Time (EST)

28 Saturday

4th ♐
Color: Indigo

29 Sunday

4th ♐
☊ D 4:13 pm
☽ v/c 6:34 pm
☽ enters ♑ 11:37 pm
Color: Amber

December/January

☽ Monday
4th ♑
New Moon 5:27 pm
Color: Gray

31 Tuesday
1st ♑
Color: Scarlet

New Year's Eve

1 Wednesday
1st ♑
☽ v/c 1:02 am
☽ enters ♒ 5:50 am
Color: Brown

New Year's Day
Kwanzaa ends

2 Thursday
1st ♒
♀ enters ♓ 10:24 pm
☽ v/c 11:13 pm
Color: Purple

Hanukkah ends

3 Friday
1st ♒
☽ enters ♓ 10:21 am
Color: Rose

Set in Eastern Standard Time (EST)

Carrot Cake

1½ cups flour
2 tsp. baking powder
½ tsp. baking soda
1 tsp. salt
1 tsp. cinnamon
4 eggs
2 tsp. vanilla extract
1 cup brown sugar
½ cup white sugar
1 cup olive oil
¼ cup butter, melted
1 lb. carrots, peeled and grated
½ cup raisins

Preheat oven to 350°F. Grease and flour an 11 × 8-inch rectangular baking dish. In a mixing bowl, sift together flour, baking powder, baking soda, salt, and cinnamon.

In a separate mixing bowl, beat eggs until foamy. Mix vanilla, sugars, oil, and butter into the eggs. Then stir in the flour mixture and mix until smooth. Mix in grated carrot and raisins. Spoon the batter into the prepared baking pan and bake for 40 to 45 minutes, or until cake springs back when touched. Let cool before serving.

Maple frosting goes well with this cake.

—Laurel Woodward

4 Saturday

1st ♓
Color: Black

Mother Earth blend is a grounding incense.

5 Sunday

1st ♓
☽ v/c 9:30 am
☽ enters ♈ 2:01 pm
Color: Yellow

About the Contributors

ELIZABETH BARRETTE was the managing editor of *PanGaia* and has been involved with the Pagan community for more than thirty years. Her book *Composing Magic* explains how to write spells, rituals, and other liturgy. She has written columns on beginning and intermediate Pagan practice, Pagan culture, and Pagan leadership. She lives in central Illinois and enjoys herbal landscaping and gardening for wildlife. Visit penultimateproductions.weebly.com and ysabet wordsmith.dreamwidth.org.

DEBORAH BLAKE is the author of over a dozen books on modern Witchcraft, including *The Little Book of Cat Magic* and *Everyday Witchcraft*, as well as the acclaimed *Everyday Witch Tarot* and *Everyday Witch Oracle*. She has also written three paranormal romance and urban fantasy series for Berkley, and her new cozy mystery series launched with *Furbidden Fatality* in 2021. Deborah lives in a 130-year-old farmhouse in Upstate New York with numerous cats who supervise all her activities, both magical and mundane.

MONICA CROSSON has been a practicing Witch and educator for over thirty years and is a member of Evergreen Coven. Monica is the author of *The Magickal Family* and *Wild Magical Soul* and is a regular contributor to Llewellyn's almanacs and datebooks as well as magazines such as *Enchanted Living* and *Witchology*. Monica lives in the woods near Concrete, Washington.

JENNIFER HEWITSON has been a freelance illustrator since 1985. Her illustrations have appeared in local and national publications, including the *Wall Street Journal*, the *Washington Post*, the *Los Angeles Times*, *US News & World Report*, and *Ladybug* magazine. Her advertising and packaging clients include Disney and the San Diego Zoo. Jennifer has created a line of greeting cards for Sun Rise Publications and has illustrated several children's books. Her work has been recognized by numerous organizations, including the Society of Illustrators of Los Angeles, and magazines such as *Communication Arts*, *Print*, and *How*.

JAMES KAMBOS is a writer and an artist from Ohio. He writes many articles on folk magic, folklore, and herbs. He tends his herb garden and paints in an American folk art style when not writing.

KELDEN (Minnesota) has been practicing Traditional Witchcraft for more than a decade. He is the author of *The Crooked Path* and *The Witch's Sabbath*. Additionally, his writing has appeared in *The Witch's Altar*, *The New Aradia*, and *This Witch* magazine. Kelden is also the cocreator of the Traditional Witch's Deck, and he authors a blog on the Patheos Pagan channel called *By Athame and Stang*. In his free time, Kelden enjoys reading, hiking, growing poisonous plants, and playing ukulele.

MICKIE MUELLER is a Witch, author, illustrator, tarot creator, and YouTube content creator. She is the author/illustrator of multiple books, articles, and tarot decks, including *Mystical Cats Tarot*, *Magical Dogs Tarot*, *The Witch's Mirror*, and *Llewellyn's Little Book of Halloween*. Her magical art is distributed internationally and has been seen as set dressing on SyFy's *The Magicians* and Bravo's *Girlfriends Guide to Divorce*. She runs several Etsy shops with her husband and fellow author Daniel Mueller in their studio workshop.

MELISSA TIPTON (Columbus, MO) is a Structural Integrator, Reiki Master, and founder of Jungian Magic, which utilizes potent psychological insights to radically increase the success of your magic. She's the author of *Llewellyn's Complete Book of Reiki* and *Living Reiki*. Visit Melissa online at http://realmagic.school/.

JD WALKER is an avid student of herbalism and gardening. She has written a regular garden column for thirty years. She is an award-winning author, journalist and magazine editor and a frequent contributor to the Llewellyn annuals. Her first book, *A Witch's Guide to Wildcrafting*, published by Llewellyn Publications, was released in spring 2021. Her new book, *Under the Sacred Canopy*, was released in early 2023.

TESS WHITEHURST (Boulder, CO) teaches magical and intuitive arts in live workshops and via her online community and learning hub, the Good Vibe Tribe Online School of Magical Arts. An award-winning author, she's written eight books, which have been translated into eighteen languages. She has appeared on the Bravo TV show *Flipping Out* as well as morning shows on both Fox and NBC, and her writing has been featured in *Writer's Digest*, in *Spirit and Destiny* (in the UK), and online at elephantjournal.com.

LAUREL WOODWARD (Portland, OR) has been a Witch for twenty years and is also a tarot reader. She has written for magazines and ezines on the subjects of healthy living, organic gardening, sustainable living, and the magick of tapping into creative energy.

Appendix

Daily Magical Influences

Each day is ruled by a planet with specific magical influences.

Monday (Moon): peace, healing, caring, psychic awareness
Tuesday (Mars): passion, courage, aggression, protection
Wednesday (Mercury): study, travel, divination, wisdom
Thursday (Jupiter): expansion, money, prosperity, generosity
Friday (Venus): love, friendship, reconciliation, beauty
Saturday (Saturn): longevity, endings, homes
Sunday (Sun): healing, spirituality, success, strength, protection

Color Correspondences

Colors are associated with each day, according to planetary influence.

Monday: gray, lavender, white, silver, ivory
Tuesday: red, white, black, gray, maroon, scarlet
Wednesday: yellow, brown, white, topaz
Thursday: green, turquoise, white, purple, crimson
Friday: white, pink, rose, purple, coral
Saturday: brown, gray, blue, indigo, black
Sunday: yellow, orange, gold, amber

Lunar Phases

Waxing, from New Moon to Full Moon, is the ideal time to do magic to draw things to you.

Waning, from Full Moon to New Moon, is a time for study, meditation, and magical work designed to banish harmful energies.

The Moon's Sign

The Moon continuously moves through each sign of the zodiac, from Aries to Pisces, staying about two and a half days in each sign. The Moon influences the sign it inhabits, creating different energies that affect our day-to-day lives.

Aries: Good for starting things. Things occur rapidly but quickly pass. People tend to be argumentative and assertive.

Taurus: Things begun now last longest, tend to increase in value, and become hard to change. Brings out an appreciation for beauty and sensory experience.

Gemini: Things begun now are easily changed by outside influence. Time for shortcuts, communication, games, and fun.

Cancer: Stimulates emotional rapport between people. Supports growth and nurturing. Tend to domestic concerns.

Leo: Draws emphasis to the self, to central ideas or institutions, away from connections with others and emotional needs.

Virgo: Favors accomplishment of details and commands from higher up. Focus on health, hygiene, and daily schedules.

Libra: Favors cooperation, compromise, social activities, balance, friendship, and partnership.

Scorpio: Increases awareness of psychic power. Precipitates psychic crises and ends connections thoroughly. People have a tendency to brood and become secretive.

Sagittarius: Encourages confidence and flights of imagination. This is an adventurous, philosophical, and athletic Moon sign. Favors expansion and growth.

Capricorn: Develops strong structure. Focus on traditions, responsibilities, and obligations. A good time to set boundaries and rules.

Aquarius: Rebellious energy. Time to break habits and make abrupt change. Personal freedom and individuality is the focus.

Pisces: The focus is on dreaming, nostalgia, intuition, and psychic impressions. A good time for spiritual or philanthropic activities.

Gemstones

Gemstones can be utilized for a variety of purposes and intentions.

Amber: ambition, balance, clarity, healing, protection, success

Amethyst: awareness, harmony, love, spirituality, protection

Citrine: beginnings, change, clarity, goals, goodness, rebirth, sleep

Emerald: clairvoyance, enchantment, jealousy, luck, spirits, wishes

Hematite: balance, grounding, knowledge, negativity, power, strength

Jade: abundance, dreamwork, money, nurture, peace, well-being, wisdom

Lodestone: attraction, fidelity, grounding, relationships, willpower

Moonstone: destiny, divination, intuition, knowledge, light, sleep

Obsidian: afterlife, aggression, death, fear, grounding, growth, obstacles

Quartz: awareness, clarity, communication, guidance, healing, rebirth

Ruby: compassion, connections, happiness, love, loyalty, passion, respect

Sapphire: astral realm, dedication, emotions, faith, improvement, insight

Tiger's Eye: battle, clarity, desire, energy, purification, strength, youth

Topaz: adaptability, courage, instrospection, loss, prosperity, wisdom

Tourmaline: attraction, business, consciousness, guidance, psychic ability

Turquoise: calm, change, creativity, dreamwork, empathy, energy, goals, healing, unity

Chakras

Chakras are spiritual energy centers located along the middle of the body.

Root Chakra: Activate with red. Balance with black.
Associated with comfort, grounding, security, support.

Sacral Chakra: Activate with orange. Balance with brown.
Associated with creativity, desire, freedom, passion.

Solar Plexus Chakra: Activate with yellow. Balance with brown.
Associated with confidence, power, transformation, willpower.

Heart Chakra: Activate with green. Balance with pink, rose.
Associated with beauty, compassion, healing, love, mindfulness.

Throat Chakra: Activate with blue. Balance with turquoise.
Associated with communication, inspiration, release, truth.

Forehead Chakra: Activate with indigo. Balance with white.
Associated with clarity, illumination, intuition, visions, wisdom.

Crown Chakra: Activate with violet, purple. Balance with gold, white.
Associated with consciousness, cosmic energy, enlightenment, knowledge, spirituality.

Herbs

Herbs are useful in spells, rituals, cooking and kitchen witchery, health, beauty, and crafts and have many common magical correspondences.

Basil: defense, home, love, prosperity, protection, purification, success

Borage: authority, business, happinesss, money, power, purification

Carnation: confidence, creativity, healing, protection, strength, truth

Chamomile: balance, beauty, calm, dreamwork, gentleness, peace, sleep

Clover: community, friendship, kindness, luck, wealth, youth

Daffodil: afterlife, beauty, faeries, fertility, luck, spirits

Daisy: beauty, cheerfulness, divination, innocence, love, pleasure

Dandelion: awareness, clarity, emotions, freedom, the mind, wishes

Fennel: aggression, courage, energy, stimulation, protection, strength

Fern: banishing, concentration, money, power, protection, release, spirits

Gardenia: comfort, compassion, the home, marriage, peace, true love

Garlic: anxiety, banishing, defense, healing, improvement, weather

Geranium: balance, concentration, fertility, forgiveness, healing

Honeysuckle: affection, gentleness, happiness, optimism, psychic ability

Ivy: animals, attachments, fertility, fidelity, growth, honor, secrets, security

Jasmine: binding, desire, dreamwork, grace, prosperity, relationships

Lavender: calm, creativity, friendship, peace, purification, sensitivity, sleep

Lilac: adaptability, beauty, clairvoyance, divination, emotions, spirits

Marigold: authority, awareness, endurance, healing, longevity, visions

Marjoram: comfort, family, innocence, loneliness, love, purification

Peppermint: action, awaken, clarity, intelligence, the mind, stimulation

Poppy: astral realm, dreamwork, fertility, luck, prosperity, sleep, visions

Rose: affection, attraction, blessings, fidelity, love, patience, sexuality

Rosemary: banishing, binding, defense, determination, healing, memory, protection

Sage: consecration, grounding, guidance, memory, obstacles, reversal

Thyme: confidence, growth, happiness, honesty, purification, sorrow

Violet: beauty, changes, endings, heartbreak, hope, lust, passion, shyness

Yarrow: awareness, banishing, calm, challenges, power, protection, success

See *Llewellyn's Complete Book of Correspondences* by Sandra Kynes for a comprehensive catalog of correspondences.

2024 Eclipses

March 25, 3:00 am; Lunar eclipse 5° ♎ 07'
April 8, 2:21 pm; Solar eclipse 19° ♈ 24'
September 17, 10:34 pm; Lunar eclipse 25° ♓ 41'
October 2, 2:49 pm; Solar eclipse 10° ♎ 04'

2024 Full Moons

Cold Moon: January 25, 12:54 pm
Quickening Moon: February 24, 7:30 am
Storm Moon: March 25, 3:00 am
Wind Moon: April 23, 7:49 pm
Flower Moon: May 23, 9:53 am
Strong Sun Moon: June 21, 9:08 pm
Blessing Moon: July 21, 6:17 am
Corn Moon: August 19, 2:26 pm
Harvest Moon: September 17, 10:34 pm
Blood Moon: October 17, 7:26 am
Mourning Moon: November 15, 4:28 pm
Long Nights Moon: December 15, 4:02 am

Planetary Retrogrades in 2024

Planet		Retrograde			Direct	
Uranus	℞	08/28/23	10:39 pm	— Direct	01/27/24	2:35 am
Mercury	℞	12/13/23	2:09 am	— Direct	01/01/24	10:08 pm
Mercury	℞	04/01/24	6:14 pm	— Direct	04/25/24	8:54 am
Pluto	℞	05/02/24	1:46 pm	— Direct	10/11/24	8:34 pm
Saturn	℞	06/29/24	3:07 pm	— Direct	11/15/24	9:20 am
Neptune	℞	07/02/24	6:40 am	— Direct	12/07/24	6:43 pm
Mercury	℞	08/05/24	12:56 am	— Direct	08/28/24	5:14 pm
Uranus	℞	09/01/24	11:18 am	— Direct	01/30/25	11:22 am
Jupiter	℞	10/09/24	3:05 am	— Direct	02/04/25	4:40 am
Mercury	℞	11/25/24	9:42 pm	— Direct	12/15/24	3:56 pm
Mars	℞	12/06/24	6:33 pm	— Direct	02/23/25	9:00 pm

Set in Eastern Time. All times corrected for Daylight Saving Time.

Moon Void-of-Course Data for 2024

JANUARY

Last Aspect Date	Time	New Sign	New Time
2	6:36 pm	2 ♎	7:47 pm
5	6:41 am	5 ♏	7:39 am
7	3:22 pm	7 ♐	4:08 pm
9	1:24 pm	9 ♑	8:33 pm
11	9:33 pm	11 ♒	10:01 pm
13	4:59 am	13 ♓	10:29 pm
15	11:33 pm	15 ♈	11:49 pm
18	3:03 am	18 ♉	3:12 am
20	8:57 am	20 ♊	8:58 am
22	3:40 pm	22 ♋	4:51 pm
24	5:58 pm	25 ♌	2:37 am
26	4:19 pm	27 ♍	2:11 pm
29	6:20 pm	30 ♎	3:04 am

FEBRUARY

Last Aspect Date	Time	New Sign	New Time
1	4:03 am	1 ♏	3:37 pm
3	10:24 pm	4 ♐	1:28 am
6	12:06 am	6 ♑	7:08 am
8	2:52 am	8 ♒	8:59 am
9	5:59 am	10 ♓	8:42 am
12	7:32 am	12 ♈	8:26 am
14	5:21 am	14 ♉	10:02 am
16	10:01 am	16 ♊	2:39 pm
18	10:21 pm	18 ♋	10:25 pm
21	1:38 am	21 ♌	8:40 am
22	11:18 pm	23 ♍	8:38 pm
26	2:35 am	26 ♎	9:29 am
27	1:22 pm	28 ♏	10:09 pm

MARCH

Last Aspect Date	Time	New Sign	New Time
2	2:47 am	2 ♐	8:56 am
4	10:41 am	4 ♑	4:15 pm
6	2:35 pm	6 ♒	7:38 pm
8	1:56 pm	8 ♓	8:03 pm
10	3:45 pm	10 ♈	8:19 pm
12	7:08 am	12 ♉	8:28 pm
14	6:29 pm	14 ♊	11:16 pm
17	12:43 am	17 ♋	5:40 am
19	2:52 pm	19 ♌	3:33 pm
22	2:34 am	22 ♍	3:42 am
24	11:49 am	24 ♎	4:37 pm
26	7:09 pm	27 ♏	5:03 am
29	11:40 am	29 ♐	3:52 pm
31	8:16 pm	4/1 ♑	12:05 am

APRIL

Last Aspect Date	Time	New Sign	New Time
3/31	8:16 pm	1 ♑	12:05 am
3	1:40 am	3 ♒	5:08 am
5	1:40 am	5 ♓	7:13 am
7	4:27 am	7 ♈	7:25 am
8	10:39 pm	9 ♉	7:23 am
11	6:04 am	11 ♊	8:59 am
13	10:46 am	13 ♋	1:45 pm
15	7:22 pm	15 ♌	10:24 pm
18	8:02 am	18 ♍	10:10 am
20	8:20 pm	20 ♎	11:08 pm
22	7:24 pm	23 ♏	11:20 am
25	7:17 pm	25 ♐	9:37 pm
28	3:31 am	28 ♑	5:37 am
30	11:19 am	30 ♒	11:20 am

MAY

Last Aspect Date	Time	New Sign	New Time
2	5:28 am	2 ♓	2:52 pm
4	3:06 pm	4 ♈	4:41 pm
6	1:57 am	6 ♉	5:42 pm
8	5:55 pm	8 ♊	7:20 pm
10	9:49 pm	10 ♋	11:13 pm
13	5:13 am	13 ♌	6:36 am
15	12:41 pm	15 ♍	5:33 pm
18	5:09 am	18 ♎	6:23 am
19	11:48 am	20 ♏	6:34 pm
23	3:28 am	23 ♐	4:24 am
25	10:47 am	25 ♑	11:36 am
27	4:02 pm	27 ♒	4:45 pm
29	10:20 am	29 ♓	8:33 pm
31	10:55 pm	31 ♈	11:28 pm

JUNE

Last Aspect Date	Time	New Sign	New Time
2	6:04 pm	3 ♉	1:55 am
5	4:09 am	5 ♊	4:36 am
7	8:16 am	7 ♋	8:41 am
9	3:05 pm	9 ♌	3:29 pm
11	3:16 pm	12 ♍	1:39 am
14	1:54 pm	14 ♎	2:12 pm
17	2:05 am	17 ♏	2:38 am
19	12:19 pm	19 ♐	12:32 pm
21	6:58 pm	21 ♑	7:08 pm
23	11:05 pm	23 ♒	11:14 pm
25	6:30 pm	26 ♓	2:08 am
28	4:45 am	28 ♈	4:52 am
30	12:56 am	30 ♉	8:00 am

JULY

Last Aspect Date	Time	New Sign	New Time
2	11:43 am	2 ♊	11:50 am
4	4:44 pm	4 ♋	4:51 pm
6	11:47 pm	6 ♌	11:56 pm
9	2:04 am	9 ♍	9:48 am
11	9:55 pm	11 ♎	10:06 pm
13	6:49 pm	14 ♏	10:53 am
16	9:10 pm	16 ♐	9:25 pm
19	3:58 am	19 ♑	4:14 am
21	7:26 am	21 ♒	7:43 am
23	5:58 am	23 ♓	9:23 am
25	10:31 am	25 ♈	10:52 am
26	6:14 pm	27 ♉	1:23 pm
29	4:59 pm	29 ♊	5:28 pm
31	10:46 pm	31 ♋	11:19 pm

AUGUST

Last Aspect Date	Time	New Sign	New Time
3	6:31 am	3 ♌	7:10 am
5	11:16 am	5 ♍	5:17 pm
8	4:40 am	8 ♎	5:31 am
10	5:45 pm	10 ♏	6:34 pm
13	5:01 am	13 ♐	6:01 am
15	12:52 pm	15 ♑	1:51 pm
17	4:43 pm	17 ♒	5:45 pm
19	2:26 pm	19 ♓	6:52 pm
21	5:54 pm	21 ♈	7:02 pm
23	8:44 pm	23 ♉	8:00 pm
25	9:40 pm	25 ♊	11:04 pm
28	3:14 am	28 ♋	4:47 am
30	11:24 am	30 ♌	1:09 pm

SEPTEMBER

Last Aspect Date	Time	New Sign	New Time
1	8:25 pm	1 ♍	11:48 pm
4	12:06 pm	4 ♎	12:12 pm
7	1:08 am	7 ♏	1:18 am
9	1:11 pm	9 ♐	1:26 pm
11	8:21 pm	11 ♑	10:38 pm
14	3:35 am	14 ♒	3:53 am
16	1:04 am	16 ♓	5:39 am
18	5:02 am	18 ♈	5:24 am
20	4:39 am	20 ♉	5:03 am
22	6:14 am	22 ♊	6:24 am
24	7:59 am	24 ♋	10:50 am
26	6:12 pm	26 ♌	6:47 pm
28	11:36 pm	29 ♍	5:42 am

OCTOBER

Last Aspect Date	Time	New Sign	New Time
1	5:39 pm	1 ♎	6:20 pm
4	6:40 am	4 ♏	7:22 am
6	6:52 pm	6 ♐	7:34 pm
9	1:54 am	9 ♑	5:38 am
11	11:53 am	11 ♒	12:31 pm
13	10:11 am	13 ♓	3:55 pm
15	4:00 pm	15 ♈	4:34 pm
17	3:26 pm	17 ♉	4:00 pm
19	3:33 pm	19 ♊	4:07 pm
21	5:00 pm	21 ♋	6:50 pm
24	12:47 am	24 ♌	1:24 am
26	4:04 pm	26 ♍	11:47 am
28	11:54 pm	29 ♎	12:30 am
31	12:57 pm	31 ♏	1:29 pm

NOVEMBER

Last Aspect Date	Time	New Sign	New Time
3	12:51 am	3 ♐	1:19 am
5	5:23 am	5 ♑	10:17 am
7	5:38 pm	7 ♒	5:58 pm
9	7:23 pm	9 ♓	11:00 pm
12	1:13 am	12 ♈	1:26 am
14	1:50 am	14 ♉	1:59 am
16	2:03 am	16 ♊	2:09 am
17	11:09 pm	18 ♋	3:50 am
20	6:20 am	20 ♌	8:51 am
22	8:15 am	22 ♍	6:01 pm
25	12:35 am	25 ♎	6:20 am
27	4:14 am	27 ♏	7:21 pm
30	1:19 am	30 ♐	6:53 am

DECEMBER

Last Aspect Date	Time	New Sign	New Time
2	10:47 am	2 ♑	4:09 pm
4	6:34 pm	4 ♒	11:21 pm
6	7:01 pm	7 ♓	4:49 am
9	3:45 am	9 ♈	8:38 am
10	5:13 pm	11 ♉	10:55 am
13	7:39 am	13 ♊	12:22 pm
15	9:32 am	15 ♋	2:21 pm
17	1:33 pm	17 ♌	6:39 pm
20	12:19 am	20 ♍	2:37 am
22	8:27 am	22 ♎	2:08 pm
24	5:44 am	25 ♏	3:06 am
27	9:24 am	27 ♐	2:46 pm
29	6:34 pm	29 ♑	11:37 pm

Set in Eastern Time. All times corrected for Daylight Saving Time.

165

Notes

Notes

Notes